Love and Wisdom

CREATIVE MULTIVERSE: NEW EXPLORATIONS IN TRANSFORMATIVE LEARNING AND RESEARCH

There is an epochal challenge of learning from multiple experiments in self and social transformations now. *Creative Multiverse* seeks to explore and present different pathways of transformations in societies and histories around the world. It builds upon engagements in learning in different disciplines of life and academy and seeks to create a transdisciplinary space of research, dialogues and transformations.

A Series from Shipra Publications, Delhi
Email: info@shiprapublications.com

LOVE AND WISDOM

Towards a New Philosophy of Life

W. JULIAN KORAB-KARPOWICZ

SHIPRA

Other Books in the Series

- A Revolutionary in Education Kristen Kold—A Pioneer of Danish Folk High School Movement
  —*Chitta Ranjan Das* (Translated by Ananta Kumar Giri)
- Diaspora and Belief—Globalisation, Religion and Identity in Postcolonial Asia
  —*John Clammer*
- New Horizons of Critical Theory—Collective Learning and Triple Contingency
  —*Piet Strydom*
- Benedict Spinoza—An Appreciation
  —*Chitta Ranjan Das*

ISBN: 978-81-7541-453-2

First Published in India in 2011

Love and Wisdom: Towards a New Philosophy of Life

Published by:

SHIPRA PUBLICATIONS

H.O.: LG 18-19, Pankaj Central Market, Patparganj,
I.P. Ext., Delhi-110092, Tel: 91-11-2223 5152, 2223 6152
Br.Off.: 4617/18, Ansari Road, Darya Ganj,
New Delhi-110002, Tel: 6594 6453, 9810522367
E-mail: info@shiprapublications.com
www.shiprapublications.com

The simplest art is life:
It is the closest to us and not unfamiliar to anyone.
But this art has been largely forgotten today
and sometimes even forbidden.

Foreword

Dare to be wise! It is energy and courage that are required to combat the obstacles which both indolence of nature and cowardice of heart put in the way of our true enlightenment [..] It is not then enough to say that all enlightenment of the understanding is worthy of respect only inasmuch as it reacts upon character. To a certain extent, it also proceeds from character, since the way to the head must be opened through the heart. *The development of man's capacity for feeling is, therefore, the more urgent need of our age, not merely because it can be a means of making better insights effective for living, but precisely because it provides the impulse for bettering our insights.*

Frederich Schiller (1982), *On the Aesthetic Education of Man*, p. 53 (emphases added).

[..] Knowing or coming to understand others requires an aspect of renunciation, a capacity for loss of self-interest and preoccupation with oneself, of overcoming narcissism [..] *to know the other in the sense of the loving care requires upon our part a movement of the whole personality towards the mode of emergence; it involves an overcoming of the selfprotective mechanism of embeddeness* [..] even to know animals in the sense of intimate rapport with them may require this sense of self-transformation. In terms of field experience, we have the exemplary research of Jane Goodall, but on a more abstract philosophical plane, we have Buber's framework of I and Thou. Buber specifically tells us that it is possible to respond to an animal as "thou"; to this we now add that it is only in so far as we do so, do we seem capable of knowing the animal and not merely have a lot of information about it. *Here again love is the condition of knowledge; indeed with this idea coming to us from animal studies, we can return enriched to the themes and problems of theology; we could now simply say that God is all-knowing because He loves all.*

R. Sunder Rajan (1998), *Beyond the Crises of European Sciences: New Beginnings*, pp. 80-81 (emphases added).

Not long before his death in June 2007, Richard Rorty wrote a piece called "The Fire of Life" in which he meditates on being diagnosed with pancreatic cancer and speaks of the consolations of poetry. He concludes: "I now wish that I had spent somewhat more of my life with verse. This is not because I fear having missed our truths that are incapable of statement in prose [..] Rather it is because I would have lived more fully if I had been able to rattle off more old chestnuts—just as I would have if I had more close friends.

I take Rorty to be saying something more than that poetry and friendship provide pleasure. He is saying that they carry us across the threshold of life or the self into richer and stranger regions than any we have known alone.

Michael D. Jackson (2010),
"The Philosopher Who Would Not Be King," p. 27.

Love and Wisdom: Towards a New Philosophy of Life brings together many of the heart-touching and evocative essays of W. Julian Korab-Karpowicz, an inspiring seeker of our times. These essays touch upon themes of love, wisdom, wonder, democracy, freedom, power, justice, international relations and oneness of all. *Love and Wisdom* urges us to nurture our multiple sources of wisdom, for example, the immortal works of Socrates, Plato, Empedocles, Thucydides and Herclitus in Greek traditions, Hugo Grotius (1583-1645) in modern Europe who did not take the short cut of Machievellian defense of state to wage war but defended rule of law in international relations, and social movements such as Solidarity from Poland, which mobilized non-violently to challenge communist dictatorship and contributed to moving beyond the Iron Curtain and to the fall of Soviet communism. *Love and Wisdom* also urges us to be on the path of spiritual awakening and along the way to rethink and reconstitute our self, society, world and modes of world-making such as myth, philosophy and science.

It is a joy for us to have *Love and Wisdom: Towards a New Philosophy of Life* in our book series, *Creative Multiverse.* It is heartening that it follows the illuminating work on the great philosopher Spinoza by Chitta Ranjan Das in our series. *Creative Multiverse* is not just a book series; it is an adventure of ideas as well as relationships. We co-travelers in this adventure get woven with each other through both wandering and wondering. I recall the cold afternoon at the Goethe Institute, Berlin in March 2006 when while searching for works on Heidegger on the internet I came across an article of Julian Korab-Karpowicz. I immediately emailed Julian who at that time was teaching philosophy and international relations at Bilkent University, Anakara, Turkey. Julian kindly invited me to visit him and Bilkent and we spent a week together in December 2006. It is during this period that I first read some of the writings of Julian and was struck by "Logos and

Wonder" which is included in this book . We then nurtured the project of a book bringing some of these illuminating and evocative essays together. We are grateful to the flow and grace of life and particularly to Mr. D Kumar of Shipra Publications and his team for enabling us to present this book as a humble gift to humanity for rethinking philosophy, science and knowledge and for cultivating love, wisdom and wonder in this broken world of ours.

Love and Wisdom is a passionate appeal for weaving threads of flowers among our broken fragments, bodies and souls and to weave a new garland of wholeness which is not totalizing but creative. It calls upon us to be new artists of life, to do threadworks of love and seeking in place of the threat works of violence and hatred. As the book urges us to realize: "Let Love at last replace Hate and Strife for there is nothing more precious than Love and Life." But *Love and Wisdom* urges us to cultivate love taking into consideration the complexities of life such as war and violence. But acknowledging reality does not mean surrendering to it. As Korab-Karpowicz tells us, Thucydides in his *History of the Peloponnesian War*, recognizes the reality of selfishness but does not exalt nor present it as a value. Similarly Hugo Grotius during the early days of European modernity takes a position against Machiavelli and argues against the reason of the state to launch war for its own sake and defends the rule of law in international relations.

Love and Wisdom urges us to celebrate love and life and in the process transform the project of our engagement with self and the world, most notably our available modes of philosophical engagement. It is said that in his last dream Socrates was "commanded to make music" (Abbs 1994: 39). "It is as if the philosopher is being invited to confront not what he has achieved in his life, but what he has neglected, even suppressed" (ibid: 39). We find in the Dialogues of Plato how Socrates is spending his "last hours turning one of Aesop's fables into verse and composing a hymn to Apollo" (ibid). Socrates is composing a hymn and Rorty expresses (as of the opening epigraphs) his desire for poetry and friendship and through this to wander in and wonder about many webs of hitherto unrealized realms and relationships.

It is in our multiple wandering and wondering with love and care that we can find ourselves, come out of our slumber and embrace each other with love and wisdom and weave threads of connections and communication in this fragile world of ours. *Love and Wisdom* inspires us for undertaking walks in wandering and wondering in soulful togetherness and pregnant solitude. We hope that this embraces many more seeking souls of our world and help us come out of our contemporary slumber, cynicism and proclivity for violence and hatred and strive for love and wisdom

Ananta Kumar Giri
Madras Institute of Development Studies

Sishsu Divas
Children's Day
Nov. 14, 2010.

REFERENCES CITED

Abbs, Peter. 1994. *The Educational Imperative: A Defense of Socratic and Aesthetic Learning.* London: The Falmer Press.

Jackson, Michael D. 2010. "The Philosopher Who Would Not Be King." *Harvard Divinity Bulletin* 38 (Nos 3-4): 20-31.

Schiller, Frederich. 1982. *On the Aesthetic Education of Man.* Oxford: Clarendon Press.

Sunder Rajan, R. 1998. *Beyond the Crises of European Sciences: New Beginnings.* Shimla: Indian Institute of Advanced Studies.

Preface

The twenty-first century is an age of a profound and rapid transformation. The new world is approaching; the old is finishing. Not only there is a shift of power from the West to the East, but also there is a complete change of values and life-styles. Customs and traditions that have animated societies for many centuries have now reached the stage of virtual extinction. There is hardly any corner of the world that has been untouched by modern technology or escaped from commercial exploitation. As human beings move forward to obtain more and more goods, they forget their true, deeper selves. They live superficially. They imagine themselves to be awake, but in fact they sleep away their lives. Especially in this time it is worth recalling the sages of old, the ancient philosophers, who urge us: Awaken. Open your eyes. Look deeper into your own self. You are not just a perishable body, but an immortal soul.

The call to the spiritual awakening is present in the early Greek thinkers to whom we refer here. Empedocles describes the evolution of the universe as animated by the two cosmic forces of Love and Hate. We can learn from him the wisdom of Love. It is

Love that brings all things into One, in the prime of flourishing Life. When Love presides among people, all things diversify and multiply, constituting nevertheless one harmonious whole—a cosmos, a unity in diversity. However, through the hostile force of Hate, each element of diversity, each human being in particular, moves apart from this harmonious whole. The fullness of Life, whose expression is the idea of unity in diversity, is also present in Heraclitus. His main concept is Logos. It is by listening to the Logos that we can experience a unity of All in One. Although the Logos may reveal itself in a way of speech, it is not just a thought. The Logos can be found in poetry and music, and above all in Nature. In the Logos, Life comes to belong to what is heard: our own being in the world.

For the people of antiquity, Nature or the world as a whole was something alive, magical and divine, which was revealed in their myths and in which they were engaged. Philosophy was born when their mythical world-view started to break down, and they were separated from Nature. The ancient Greek philosophers tried to prevent their contemporaries from losing their engagement with the world. The function of philosophy at the early stage was still similar to that of myth, revealing the meaning of the whole and directing human behavior. Ancient thinkers emphasized the importance of virtue and moral uprightness. Only in the 17th century was the classical moral tradition that developed in the West from Platonic and Aristotelian philosophies challenged by modern thought. In the philosophies of Hobbes and Locke, human beings are reduced to soulless, desire-driven, self-interested individuals. Subjected to countless desires, they begin to identify themselves with their bodies and lose their devotional and affective engagement with the world. The world becomes an object of, on the one hand, disinterested scientific inquiry and, on the other hand, of merciless commercial exploitation. Modernity thus overturns the ideas and values of the traditional culture of the West, and, once it becomes global, leads to the erosion of other traditional cultures. The further destruction of traditional thinking and ways of life is brought about by post-modernity, which represents a challenge to modernity, but at the same time is a radical continuation of the modern project.

In order to reverse these pernicious developments – the destruction of natural environment and of traditional cultures – today's philosophy must recognize the illusion on which modernity stands. As the love of wisdom, philosophy presupposes being engaged with the world rather than being indifferent or exploitative. A positive social change can only occur if by love human separateness is overcome, and if there is freedom from hate. Life is a central category around which human beings can unify. However, life is not merely about physiological processes. Human life includes full psychological development, and this can be achieved only in certain conditions. The Global Solidarity which is indispensible for the solution of today's immense world problems depends on the recognition of some fundamental human needs. It relies on the growing understanding of what is right for life. It is based on the righteousness of life.

The essays collected in this book were written between 1985 and 2009. They seem all different, and yet they are interconnected by the ideas of Love, Wisdom, Philosophy and Life. I am deeply indebted to Dr Ananta Kumar Giri, editor of the book series, for encouraging me to rewrite them and to put them together for the purpose of this collection.

I am grateful to the editors and publishers for permission to reprint the following chapters.

Chapter 1 was originally published under the title "The Wisdom of Love: A Reflection Upon Empedocles' Fragment 35, Philosophy, War, and Peace," *Dialectics and Humanism*, 17.3 (1990).

Chapter 3 was originally first published under the title "Rethinking Philosophy: A Reflection on Philosophy, Myth, and Science," *Philosophy Today*, 46.2 (2002).

Chapter 4 is a revised text of my article entitled "Knowing Beyond Science: What Can We Know and How Can We Know?", *Humanitas*, 15.2 (2002).

Chapter 5 is a revised text of my article entitled "On the Power of Virtue: Universalism of Plato's Political Philosophy," *Dialogue and Universalism*, 13.7-8 (2003).

Chapter 6 was originally published under the title "How International Relations Theorists Can Benefit by Reading Thucydides," *The Monist*, 89.2 (April 2006).

Chapter 7 was originally published under the title "In Defense of International Order: Grotius' Critique of Machiavellism," *The Review of Metaphysics* 60.1 (September 2006).

Chapter 8 is a revised text of my article entitled "Freedom from Hate: Solidarity and Nonviolent Political Struggle in Poland" printed in *Journal of Human Values*, vol. 8.1 (2002).

Chapter 9 is a revised article published under the title "On the Righteousness of Life: Global Solidarity Values for the 21st Century," *Dialogue and Universalism*, 19. 11-12 (2009).

Contents

I. The Wisdom of Love

Love must you contemplate with your mind and not just sit with your eyes dazed. —*Empedocles*

Let me speak today. Let me come into my own. This is a Symposium, a place of intercourse of ideas between people. Let me then speak.[1]

Firstly, I shall tell you why I may speak. When I began my studies in philosophy, a professor who taught courses on the early Greeks once said to me that in the Pythagorean School the students were supposed to be quiet for four years before they could speak. Respecting the advice of my teacher, I was quiet even longer, for six years. But now it is over seven years ago since I began to study philosophy, and the number seven symbolizes completeness. So this is why I may speak and do not need merely to repeat.

Seven wise men, it is believed, once lived in Greece. There were seven wonders in the ancient world. By the seventh day the world had been completed. So too I have been completed as a philosopher by the seventh year. Yet, Philosophy as such has not been completed, and I believe she will not be completed as long as she is Philosophy.

Philosophy will never be completed. One can be completed as a philosopher, but a philosopher is one who by definition is not completed. A philosopher is a lover of Wisdom. Only ifÿÿe is united in love with Wisdom does he reach completeness. However, as a mere philosopher he is not completed. He needs Wisdom, and the union of a philosopher and Wisdom constitutes completeness.

The union of a philosopher with Wisdom bears fruit. The fruit of the love between a philosopher and Wisdom is Philosophy. However, Philosophy, although a child of completeness, is herself not completed simply because she grows up. Perhaps she might be completed, yet then she does not signify the love of Wisdom, but becomes Wisdom herself, and is not Philosophy anymore. Philosophy when completed becomes Wisdom, but again Wisdom as such is also not completed. Wisdom needs a philosopher to reach completeness.

Consequently, a philosopher as a human being is incomplete in himself; rather he is desirous of Wisdom, and so moves towards completeness. Philosophy, the fruit of love between a philosopher and Wisdom, is also not completed, as long as she is Philosophy.

Parmenides, desirous of Wisdom, was carried from the kingdom of night, where we mortals presently dwell, to the kingdom of day where Truth, the goddess, dwells. He came to her so as to listen to her. However, he was too young to know that one should not only to listen to Truth, but also love Truth, for this is the way to know. She received him kindly, but just as he came to her as a youth, so also he returned to the kingdom of night as a youth, and not as a man.

The quest for Truth is indeed very much bound with the erotic. The love of Wisdom and the quest for Truth are results of the incompleteness of the one who is the lover and the searcher.

Nevertheless, as it is recounted in the tale, Parmenides returned from his journey as a youth. He was a mere listener to Truth – not her lover. This is why he repeats after the goddess what she says about a path "that is not and that is needful that it not be".[2] The goddess tells him that this path of inquiry cannot be explored, as it is not possible to know what is unknown. Indeed, he was too young to know Love, and the unknown was not revealed to him.

There is always an unknown for a philosopher because he is not completed, and only one who is fully completed may know the presently unknown. However, even the gods are not completed. They need a world to rule and to care for to be completed. The gods are like those human beings who have such a rich and abundant spirit that they need Matter to express this spirit. They are like those brilliant artists, who when completed as artists, are still not completed in themselves because they can manifest their genius only through Matter. They create because they are so rich in their sprit that they have to express it in a variety of forms, sounds, and colors.

God united with the world constitutes completeness. When the gods rule, united in Love with the Earth they govern, a Golden Age comes into being on this planet. Like painters who take many-colored pigments, mix them in harmony and paint the forms of all things, the gods fecundate the Earth, so that she brings forth a countless diversity of life-forms.

When a society is ruled by a divine government, in accordance with the law of Nature, then almost all things have the unique and unprecedented character of an individual. Cities and villages are all different from each other. Crafts, and not mass production, flourish. In such a time, one can encounter on the street a colorful mosaic of human types. It is a time of "unity in diversity" in Love. Things diversify and multiply, constituting nevertheless one Whole, a cosmos. Astrologers trace with great care the paths of the stars, so as to foresee any danger that might end this Golden Age.

Now, when the four basic elements – out of which, according to Empedocles, the All, including the gods, is constituted – mingle, "countless tribes of mortal things pour forth, filled with forms of all kinds, a wonder to look upon."[3] This happens when Love dominates and melds this diversity into the one, ordered Whole.[4] At other times, however, each element of diversity, each human being in particular, moves apart from this harmonious Whole through the hostile force of Hate. Then each element stands in opposition to the others. There is separation, chaos, strife; there is no longer a cosmos, an ordered Whole.

The four elements – air, fire, earth, and water – were recognized long before Empedocles and other ancient Greek philosophers as the basic components of the living phenomenal world. In order to appreciate fully what Empedocles says, we have to realize that the number four traditionally symbolized the Earth, the World, or the Whole. The four elements constitute the Whole not merely in the material, but also, more significantly, in the symbolic sense. When the four elements come into being, a cosmos is constituted. Consequently, Empedocles speaks about the evolution of the world-which-is, at least in the form of the four imperishable elements. He does not speak about that which is not, namely, about the chaos out of which these elements separated themselves. The Chaos, which preceded our world, comes into view as the unknown about which one does not speak as long it remains unknown.

The notions of chaos and cosmos may be applied to different situation. We can say that a country is in chaos because strife is occurring there, and that a statesman whishes to bring that country (a cosmos) back to its proper, ordered state. The same applies to the organic world. When the basic components mingle together in Love, then they may constitute a beautiful flower or a human being. However, when the right time comes, everything that is mortal dissolves back to chaos.

There is always a cosmos at a higher plane of the universe that evolves, so long as it does not dissolve itself, by going through the changes of *cosmoi* at the lower planes. Further, in the Whole or in the World, there is already contained something that makes evolution possible – evolution through Love, leading to creation, and also evolution through Hate, leading to destruction. That which makes this possibility is Eros.

Long ago Hesiod said that Eros is "the most beautiful of immortal gods who in every man and in every god softens the sinews and overcomes the prudent purpose of the mind".[5] However, what Hesiod does not tell us here is that Love is only one manifestation of Eros and that there is another manifestation as well: Strife. Eros may lead us to Love, but also to Hate and Strife.[6] Nevertheless, it is Eros who, although as such incomplete, leads the Whole to evolve, and makes people love each other, and acquire knowledge.

In fact, we can trace the origin of Eros back to the four elements. When Heraclitus says that "the ordered universe was not created by any one of the gods or men but it was ever and is and shall be ever-living Fire,"[7] he describes his conception of the universe as being in the state of endless evolution and transformation. This is also why he says that Strife is just.[8] He does not praise strife among people, strife manifested as violent and unnecessary domestic or international conflict. What he suggests is that Strife, the manifestation of Hate, is a component of the Whole. So, we can add that Love is also such a component. Consequently, the origin of Eros can be traced to Fire – to a power that is both creative and destructive. It is Eros who orders the universe. He is not a man or a god. But, if we consider him a god, Eros is the most beautiful of immortal gods when he is manifested in Love.

Through Love, All comes together into One. The One, the Whole or the cosmos, grows into one from many. In the Age of

Love, All is united in Love and forms the One, a unity in diversity. On the other hand, through the hatred of Strife, each element is carried apart. In the Age of Strife, the whole dissolves into many separate entities that are in strife with each another.[9]

One can say that the cosmic evolution of Empedocles, which proceeds from the Age of Love to the Age of Strife, back to the Age of Love, and so on, ultimately applies to the whole universe. Indeed, this evolution can be traced on countless planes.

After the day comes the night, and after this night comes another day. The day reveals to us the manifold diversity of forms, sounds, and colors, that constitutes a cosmos, a unity in diversity; the night in turn obscures all this, so that we need to strike a light in order to see anything during the night. Does the day represents the Age of Love, and the night, the Age of Strife? In fact, the night is also a time during which lovers are brought together, and in the day separateness of things seems much more apparent then their unity, so that all this is not as easy to distinguish as it at first seems.

However, I will not attempt to inquire into the evolution of the universe. Empedocles himself concentrates only on that-which-is, on the world that does not completely dissolve into chaos and perish because the world-that-is persists at least in the form of the four separable and imperishable elements. This is why I do not wish to speak here about the night. In the night, the elements are not distinguished and everything that the day reveals perishes. Therefore, let me again concentrate on the world-that-is, on the living and phenomenal world of which human beings are themselves components.

Let us locate ourselves somewhere on the circle of evolution. Just like the ancient Greeks we no longer live in a Golden Age. The Golden Age occurs when a society is regulated by a myth, and is ordered and ruled by a divine government. At such a time people are *engaged* in the world, of which the myth and the society are integral parts. They love their world. Like children who do not complain about the differences that divide them from their parents and other adults, the inhabitants of a mythological society, all knowing their own places, do not question their difference because there is Love between them. They live in harmony with their society, and do not wish to change it or revolt against it.

Today, as the ancient Greeks already did so long ago, we live in the Age of Iron. The Greeks were the pioneers of the early Iron Age. This is why they still cherished the memory of the Golden Age of Chronos. Nevertheless, their age was not golden anymore, but iron, and this is why they developed philosophy: to replace the corrupted myths that could not regulate their society any longer.[10]

Obviously the Age of Iron takes its name from iron. Let us reflect on the nature of gold and iron. Gold reminds us of the Sun. It is the symbol and reflection of the divine Sun on our worldly world, just as beautiful jewelry can remind us of the brightness of the stars. In contrast, iron was initially developed for the sake of making swords. Thus, we know how the Iron Age began – it began with war. We, like the ancient Greeks and all who came between us, live in an age of war.

Accordingly, the Iron Age is one of the successive manifestations of the Age of Strife. However, we are not at the beginning of this age. Today, the diversity of life-forms is disappearing as more quickly then ever before. The world has become almost as one community that is divided into hostile elements in strife with each other. Diversity in unity does not prevail in this world; instead, separation into huge, hostile powers seems to have become the political reality. In spite of the efforts aimed to promote multiculturalism, the mosaic of human types and ways of living, like the variety of dialects and languages, is disappearing. The movement away from diversity and towards uniformity even goes as far as attempting to dismiss the fundamental difference that makes the evolution of the universe possible, namely, the difference between man and woman. To dismiss this difference, which is a basic feature of the universe, is to get rid of Eros. But those who fight against Eros, are, consciously or not, *in* Eros because Eros does not only lead to Love, but also to Strife. They, nevertheless, do not choose Love, "the most beautiful of immortal gods," but rather Strife and destruction. Thus we stray further and further from the Golden Age.

This is Science, which eases human lives and makes them more prosperous. Unfortunately, it is also Science that causes people to forget about Eros. Science does not look at things with affection but rather with indifference, as if they were objects. Even when Science speaks about Eros, she describes the latter as an object, so that she in fact overlooks Eros.

At the beginning of the Iron Age there was no Science. Then, a child was born to replace the elderly and corrupted Myth, namely, Philosophy. Philosophy is never completed. She brings about the desire for completion, and requires her lovers to be completed. Like Wisdom, she opens her gates only to those who are her lovers. Philosophy is not open to those who do not love her. When one loves Philosophy, one becomes her child, a philosopher. The gates to Wisdom are open only to her lovers, to philosophers, not to anyone else. By contrast, the gates of Science are open to everyone, because Science does not care. She is indifferent.

We are not at the beginning of the Iron Age, but at its very end. There are so many people today who choose to replace love with their narrow concept of justice and philosophy with science. They do not realize that this is the beginning of the end and that there might be deadly Strife ahead of us.

More than a half century has now passed since we released ourselves from the last world war, bloody and foolish strife in which iron tanks, ships and planes battled each other. Nevertheless, people were also present there, and because of this, it was still in a sense a "human" war. The soldiers not only fought against their enemies, but they also heard the beating of their fellows' hearts when they were brought together at the front. And when they came back, they kissed their women, and told them it was impossible there would ever be war again. And then I was born. So, now you know where I am from: I am from the country that is the heart of Love and war.

There might be Strife ahead of us, but should it come it would be less "human" than the last one. There would be no battle front. Machines would fight against each other, and there would be no kisses afterwards for then we all dissolve into the elements. But let me quote Empedocles now:

When Hate has reached the bottommost abyss of the eddy, and when Love reaches the middle of the whirl, then in the whirl all these things come together so as to be One – not at once, but voluntarily uniting, some from one quarter, others from another. And as they mix, there pour forth countless races of mortals.[11]

The world, like a ship, sails through the universe, and we might have deadly Strife, a dreaded reef, ahead of us, but at least it can be seen from afar. So, before those who still belong to the Iron Age make a last attempt to destroy our world, which has already begun its transition to a new age, the Intelligence Age, let us turn away from Strife. Let Love at last replace Hate and Strife for there is nothing more precious than Love and Life.

Postscript Comments by Edward Hussey, Fellow, All Souls College, Oxford

The cosmic cycle of Empedocles, which is the starting point for the reflections of Prof. W. J. Korab-Karpowicz, has been much discussed. The key to a correct understanding lies in the correct conception of the characteristic activities of Love and Strife respectively.

Empedocles, as Korab-Karpowicz remarks, sees both Love and Strife as forces active on many levels and scales. But they are the same forces throughout. Everywhere their activities are essentially the same. That of Love is not merely to bring together unlike things, but to strip them of their mutually opposed properties, to assimilate them to one another, to fuse them into a homogeneous compound. That of Strife, on the contrary is to break up such compounds, and to reduce them into mutually hostile ingredients. Empedocles sees these as the two great forces that are at work in the cosmos, at the properly cosmic level, at the level of political and personal life, and at the level of "chemistry."

The two forces alternate, locally and cosmically; and hence, there is a long-term cosmic cycle in which the universe as a whole passes from a state of complete union, under Love, through the period of increasing Strife to an extreme state of disaggregation in which the warring elements exist each as itself, in total opposition to all the others; and then back again through the stages of ever greater unification to the domination of Love again. But where in all this is there room for the familiar world that we know? This exhibits both unification and disunification: there are plenty of chemical compounds, organic unities, families and societies, but also plenty of difference and opposition. Without this combination of unification and difference, our world would not exist. So it is possible only in the two intermediate stages of the cycle: when Strife is increasing but has not yet completely replaced Love, and when Strife is repeating but has not yet completely yielded to Love. This explains the fragile, transitory and compromised nature of goodness in this ordinary world.

Empedocles, through he is a determinist about the history of the cosmos, is not a determinist about the fate of the individual. At this level, it is clear, the individual has the choice: to expel strife from her or his being, or to let it grow strong there. The being which keeps itself full of love will automatically be united with the cosmic Love, even if this is temporarily exiled from the cosmos. The being that is torn by strife will be made to circulate in the cosmic battleground of Strife, and will be all but torn to pieces in itself. Empedocles's physical causation, mediated by the purpose of "like to like," ensures appropriate destinies for each kind of being. The physical cosmos, as known by human science, is for Empedocles at the same time a moral cosmos: indeed there is no essential distinction for him between physical and moral science, or between ethics and politics. It is this darling attempt to reach a unified understanding of the universe that is the starting-point for the reflections of Korab-Karpowicz on "The Wisdom of Love".[12]

NOTES

1. This text was originally presented at a graduate philosophy seminar at the Catholic University of America in the spring of 1985 and first published under the title "The Wisdom of Love: A Reflection Upon Empedocles' Fragment 35, Philosophy, War, and Peace," *Dialectics and Humanism* No. 3/1990, pp. 211-216.
2. Parmenides, fragment 2. All sayings of the early Greek thinkers quoted in this book are numbered according to the standard numeration of the later editions of Diels-Kranz (H. Diels, *Die Fragmente der Vorsokratiker*, 6th and later editions, ed. W. Kranz).
3. Empedocles, fragment 35.
4. Empedocles, fragment 26
5. See Hesiod, *Theogony*.
6. The kinship between Eros and Strife is revealed to us by Homer in the *Illiad*. Eros is manifested in Love as the desire for unity in diversity, and manifested in Strife as the selfish desire that is destructive of all diversity.

7. Heraclitus, fragment 30.
8. See Heraclitus, fragment 80.
9. Empedocles, fragments 17 and 26.
10. See Chapter "Rethinking Philosophy."
11. Empedocles, fragment 35.
12. This text was originally published under the title "Comments on W. J. Korab-Karpowicz's 'Wisdom of Love'," *Dialectics and Humanism* No. 3/1990, pp. 231-232.

2. Logos and Wonder

> One thing is wise: to understand the thought by which all things are steered by all things. – *Heraclitus*

When Heraclitus asks us to listen to the Logos, he at the same time cautions us not to listen to him, or to his talking. If we are too much attached to the meanings of individual words we may overlook the wholeness which is created by them: we may overlook the thought of which the words are component parts. Caught up in studying elements or parts, we may overlook the whole. But the Logos is not a thought, although it may reveal itself that way in speech. The Logos can reveal itself *in* us, even in such a form, for example, as the sound of the ocean. In such a case, it is no longer a thought. It can then be repeated to others only by a poet or a composer, because only they can repeat what the ocean says in them.

Music and poetry, when great and when heard, embrace, surround and enter us, so that we are not separated from them anymore. Attuned to them, we can reveal *in* us the meaning of the human-being-in-this-world, as it is for a poet or composer. If artists truly wish share with us their being, if their souls and skills are great, then we allow them to enter our space and we are no longer indifferent to them. We attune ourselves to their words and music because through them, in the Logos, Life comes to belong to that which is heard: our own very being in this world.

To find one's own being in the work of an artist is the highest mode of being engaged with art. But how it is possible to be attuned to that music and to that art in which the artists do not truly share with us their spirit? How to be engaged with that art that is meant to delude, to sale, or to be "just for fun"? How to find the Logos in today's "mass culture"? How to be engaged with all this foolishness? We can be only indifferent in such a case (a lesson in being indifferent) or, at any rate, not too serious about it. Even so, in one way or another, mass culture enters today's human beings and this is a very real loss.

Generalizations about mass culture may lead us to a misinterpretation of what is really happening in art today. There are still artists whose concern is to reveal the meaning of the human being-in-this-world, for they care about this world. What a pity it is that they are not frequent guests in our homes. But even if they do come to visit us, how can we, who are not used in engaging with art, recognize them? To distinguish the Logos from false and corrupted *logoi*, we need to open our eyes and our ears.

Finding one's-own-being-in-the-world in the work of an artist is the highest mode of being engaged with art. Unfortunately, in contemporary culture a work of art is often no more than a joke and does not deserve to be taken seriously. One needs to remember that to learn how to recognize the true Logos of art from false logos-es, we need to go where the greatest artists, who share with us everything they have, are. Further, we need to visit places where there is the poetry or music of which Nature is the composer.

And then, after experiencing such examples of true art, we will be able to discern that even in pop culture, there are occasions when something is sincerely said and touches the Logos: something that unexpectedly reveals the meaning of the human-being-in-this-world through the artist's joy and despair, love and sorrow, through his greatness.

The problem of distinguishing between the Logos and corrupted *logoi* is even harder to work through in philosophy then it is in art. We can only do this for ourselves. Here we search for the greatest not only within the Western philosophical tradition, but also beyond it. We can study the Book of Genesis, the Zend Avesta, and the sacred books of India because the wise agree with each other, and the cosmological representation that they presented at the surface level is in fact a seeming under which there is hidden something most precious: the meaning of the human-being-in-this-world that is revealed in us. After such preparation studying even Kant or the positivists can be quite an illuminating experience. We do not wish to immense ourselves in the past for its own sake alone, but rather to know the past so as to better understand the present and to have the means of comparison. If you want to attune yourself to the Logos, go to where the greatest, immortal mortals are; some of them are already a few thousand years old. Beyond this, you can go still further, and seek out Nature. She is the oldest one of all and can never mislead us. Listen to how the ocean laps at the shores, how the trees in the forest converse with each other, and how the river flows ceaselessly between its banks. They are your dear friends, if you would only take the time to understand their speech.

What Heraclitus cautions us about is again, not to take a seeming as a whole, but rather to try to be attuned to the whole. Not only words, but even paragraphs may say nothing to those who have not attuned themselves to the essential reality that underlies and reveals itself in them. This does not mean that we should not study individual words or parts. Sometimes even a word can reveal the whole: the word "Logos," for example. But when this word is casually translated and written as "measure," "law," or even "word," it is no wonder that the reader cannot grasp the whole in such an obscured version. In this and similar cases, the perceptive reader should then go back to the origin of whatever words are in question, and try to find their original meanings, and then compose the whole again, as he thinks it was meant to be.

But here I have touched on yet another problem. How do I know that what I write about Heraclitus is really what was meant by him? How do we know what he meant when he spoke about the Logos? We are looking for life among the dead. But those who have died will not tell us anymore about themselves. They will not correct our translations. However, for the sake of an exercise, imagine for a moment that Heraclitus and other ancient philosophers suddenly enter the room. We would probably find them different from the way we usually imagine them. They would not wear tunics; they would not have long white beards. They would look almost like anyone else you might encounter on the street, at work or on a bus—that is, until you looked into their eyes. There would be something different, perhaps divine about their eyes, because they can see what others cannot.

Then, you would understand who just walked into the room, and would say: "Nice to see you, Thales. What do you think about water?" or "How do you do, Heraclitus? Tell us something about the Logos." And he would answer. "Of the Logos people always prove to be uncomprehending—but first, how about giving us something to drink?" "Just a glass of water," Tales would add.

How splendid it would be if they were, indeed, with us! Unfortunately, they are not; yet, in a way, they are. However, in order to see them, we have to open our eyes. Philosophers do not necessarily have long beards, wear tunics, or write long treatises. Only those whose eyes are closed see philosophers that way and look for greatness somewhere beyond our world, in transcendence. In reality, the magnanimous individuals are not exclusively the ones who are already dead. The people around us, whom we regard as the multitude and call "the many," are not simply the many. Among the many are the few, and to see the many as the many is to overlook the few. But how often is it the case that people do not recognize the few among them, because they imagine the few in a way the few are not. The few are not a transcendent but rather an immanent part of the world, as the ancient Greeks realized.

The few can recognize the few, and then rejoice, and they know how to rejoice because they also know what grief is. Their ancient wisdom speaks to all of us: Do not look for the living among the dead, but among the living!

However, the very few have also the power to resuscitate the dead. They can resuscitate Heraclitus, for example, by making his thought alive again; and Heraclitus, the immortal mortal, is thus immortal not, indeed, in his body but in his thought. The few can make his thought live again—the thought which reveals Heraclitus's very being in this world and which makes him as close to us as if he were our contemporary—because the human-being-in-this-world, that which myth or philosophy (in the proper sense of this world) reveals, is valid forever, or at any rate for as long as there are human beings. What was apparently obscure about Heraclitus becomes clear and is transformed into the mystery of Heraclitus, as well as into the mystery of the human-being-in-this-world as such. We can then almost speak with Heraclitus as if he were alive. He becomes someone very precious to us: an old, very well known friend (if we know what it is to have friends). When philosophers present themselves to us in this way, we can say that we have entered their divine gardens, and that our eyes and ears have opened.

We will never know someone if we regard him or her as an object of misuse or purely detached investigation. Can you imagine the princes Scheherezade as an object of scientific inquiry? She might be weighted and measured all over. She might be given psychological tests. But would she be known that way? To know her we must enter the mystery of her days and nights, become her lover, mingle our sweat with her sweat. But each day she would still be new anyway and she would tell us a new story, and one day she would give birth to our children – the dear, erotic, and beautiful Scheherezade. So also is our world when it is not being destroyed.

The many are not the many because among the many we can surprisingly encounter the few. The many are also not the many because we can conceive of societies in which the many are engaged in the world and with themselves, and live in conversation with Nature. Although appearing to be "the many," they have their eyes and ears open, so that they are in fact the few and not the many. Lastly, insofar as this essay is concerned, the many are not the many because the goal here is not to offend anyone or to classify people into groups (such a classification might itself become another delusion) but rather to open the readers' eyes. My goal is not to offend even those who are so ignorant as to not understand that killing and destruction are bad. Their eyes are not merely closed, but shut down.

Those whose eyes are closed, sleep. They look like innocent sleepers. Almost no one today—at least at universities—teaches the science of awakening and practices the art of opening eyes, so that many of us sleep away their lives. The ignorant, however, do not sleep away, but die their lives. They are so separate from other people, whom they are prepared to kill, that, even when they seem to smile, no shadow of true happiness appears on their face. Perhaps they may feel good about themselves or feel pleasure in their body, but they do not have a real conception of happiness, unless they perhaps have a faint recollection of it from their childhood. If they are to become humane, they must start all over again and learn everything from the beginning, *arche*.

3. Rethinking Philosophy

All human beings by nature desire to know.

— Aristotle

What is philosophy? What is myth? What is science? None of these questions can easily be answered. Different philosophical schools define philosophy in accordance with their various philosophical standpoints. The numerous traditional stories to which the term "myth" is commonly applied cover an enormous area, so that it may be mistaken to look for some general definition of all myths. Some scientists maintain that there is no single category "science" and that a general characterization of science cannot be established.

The purpose of this essay is to establish a relationship between philosophy, myth, and science in reference to a historical perspective. If for methodological reasons we now disregard the mentioned above terminological difficulties and refer to a common-sense view of myth, philosophy, and science, it remains unquestionable that myth existed long before philosophy and modern science began as late as the seventeenth century. Nevertheless, this historical perspective is not introduced to affirm the positivistic view, according to which the history of humanity should be described in terms of three stages: theological (mythical), metaphysical (philosophical), and positive (scientific); nor is it presented to say that the positive one represents the final achievement of the human race. On the contrary, I will attempt to show that by departing from myth and original philosophy, modern men and women have concealed from themselves an intensely rich experience of life. In order to regain the love of wisdom, we need first to look backwards in order to move forward.

Myth and Its Dimensions. To some scholars myths are simply the imaginative products of a primitive mind. They are traditional stories, the narratives that are told in archaic, non-literate societies. To others, myths are sacred tales, revelatory and exemplary, because they are either literal or symbolic representations of reality and determine exemplary models of human actions. It is acknowledged that myths constitute a very complex and at the same time uncertain category.[1] I will propose a definition that will at least in part pay tribune to the complexity of myth: *myth is a wholeness attuned to the world as a whole and disclosing the world in its completeness*. In order to make this statement more clear, I need first to explain what I call "mythical attitude."[2]

"Mythical attitude" is an expression by which I characterize the way in which a member of a mythical archaic society relates to the world. It is commonly agreed upon that for the archaic human being the world is not what it is for us today. For archaic men and women the world as a whole is "thou." The world is unique and has an unprecedented character of a person, or even of a relative. Nature is the manifestation of the divine and is revered. Winds, rivers, headlands, mountains, springs, and animals are all personified and become subjects of myths. The natural world is permeated by forces which are depicted in divine and human terms.

A member of a mythical society does not feel separated from, but rather engaged with, the world. "Thou" is not intellectually reflected upon, but experienced as life meeting life.[3] Mythical attitude is thus one that can be best characterized by the word "engagement." Further, it is neither the attitude of a rational, disinterested observer nor of a self-interested hedonist, which can both be attributed to the modern individual. It is also not the attitude of a believer, based on faith.[4] It is rather the attitude of an engaged devotee or lover.

Whether it is about the creation of the world, an animal, or an institution, a myth narrates something as if it would really happen. For the archaic human being myths are true stories that concern themselves with realities.[5] Consequently, the world as "thou" reveals itself in myth firstly as a cosmological representation in which supernatural powers, miracles, and gods are believed to truly exist. This representation is real and sacred, but it is not objective. Being objective presupposes an attitude of an indifferent, neutral, and impartial observer, which is not the mythical attitude. The cosmological representation of myth is based on devotional engagement. For archaic men and women, Nature or the world as a whole is not an object, but something magic, alive, and divine. This cosmological representation, which involves supernatural powers, is neither objective nor based on faith, but is taken literally by virtue of engaged devotion. However, as soon as humans lose their devotional engagement with the world, the cosmological representation may become invalid for them. They can "objectively" disprove the existence of "thou" and all supernatural phenomena.

Myth, the result of the revelation of "thou," is always a whole. It is not created part by part. It is not a product of discursive or inductive reasoning. The ecstasy, the supreme mystical experience of the revelation, takes one beyond the realms of the sensorial and rational.[6] A sudden revelation may reveal the world as it is as a whole in a myth. It is the experience of existence in its totality that can manifest the sacred and introduce new meaningful patterns upon man's life and his world. When I say that *myth is a wholeness attuned to the world as a whole*, I mean firstly that myth, the result of the revelation of the world as a whole, is completed as a whole already at its beginning by one who is the divine knower, the mystic, the inspired shaman, the godlike mortal, its receiver and creator. It is completed already at the beginning; and yet, it evolves. But it evolves as slowly as mythological society develops; that is, very slowly in comparison to the development of modern society. We can simply acknowledge that myth's evolution proceeds from revelation to revelation. It can be stimulated by those few – the mystics – who would prove themselves to be divine knowers and who would understand the layers of meaning which constitute the wholeness of myth.

Myths are not simple and uniform. They are often multidimensional, endowed with different emphases and levels of meanings. A myth does not have mostly a fixed meaning, but a number of them. "Myth, like symbol, has its own particular 'logic,' its own intrinsic consistency which enables it to be 'true' on a variety of planes."[7] When I say that *myth is a wholeness*, I also mean all the levels or layers of meaning that can be found in myth constitute a wholeness and myths do not yield to one particular, partial interpretation. What is whole cannot be justifiably reduced to any of its parts. Yet the different levels of meaning can be discovered. Their discovery corresponds to what can be called an expansion of one's understanding or spiritual growth. Myths are sacred tales, revelatory and exemplary, because they reveal the structure of reality to the archaic human being and supply him with exemplary models for his actions. They validate every custom and institution of a mythological society.[8] But, as he grows spiritually, a member of a mythical society, the shaman or mystic is able to understand new meanings which are revealed to him in myth. Understanding is not a mere intellectual or theoretical category here. Initiated into new planes on which "thou" is revealed in myth, archaic man responds by way of his behavior and by his being.

The world as "thou" is a life presence whose qualities can be articulated because the "thou" can reveal itself. Humanity original experiences in meeting this "thou" – the experiences of existence in its totality which reveal to men and women the meaning of their being in the world – are conveyed in myths. Myth perpetuates the revelation of the "thou." The purpose of many myths is to revoke, re-establish, or to re-enact the creative era in which the original meeting of humans and the "thou" took place. The original experiences that lay at the origin of myths can thus be reclaimed. These experiences are contained in different levels or layers of meanings that can be discovered in myth, and thus, recovered. Through the interpretation of the cosmological representation of myth which is mostly symbolic, the human being can regain an understanding of himself in the world. He can disclose the meaning of his being, which is the human-being-in-this world, as well as the meaning of myth as such. When I say that *myth is a wholeness disclosing the world in its completeness*, I mean that myth is a certain interpretative unit, a unity of its different meanings that can be recovered and that can lead us back to the original experiences of humans meeting the world as a whole as "thou."

From Myth to Philosophy. Even if we accept that myths are results of the revelation of a "thou" and are often founded upon an original experience that reaches beyond the sensorial and rational, we can still maintain that they are not illogical. They are indeed mostly susceptible to rational analysis and logical interpretation. An analysis of many myths would show that actions of gods and heroes often presuppose a keen analysis of given circumstances and are based on rational decisions.[9] At least we can say that some myths represent complex logical systems that are different from those that are usually found in contemporary Western societies. Yet, according to a common view, there is a radical separation between *muthos* and *logos*, between myth and philosophy. Myth is associated with the mysterious and illogical, and philosophy with the rational and logical. Myths are part of a way of life and state precedence and models for human actions, but unlike philosophy they do not seek to explain them on a rational basis. Myths use images; philosophy, concepts. Philosophy asks generalized questions, relies on systematic reasoning, and rejects the supernatural explanations of the world, but myths are usually confined to a particular mythological society, are unsystematic and deal with the sacred.

The beginning of philosophy is not the result of one brief shining moment of a sudden discovery of a rational, philosophical mind. Only on a very superficial interpretation are myths illogical and deprived of rational thinking. The emergence of philosophy in Greece was preceded by the rationalizing and systematizing of myths, such as we can find, for example, in Hesiod's *Theogony.*[10] The process by which myth gave way to philosophy is thus far from straightforward, extending over several centuries. Nevertheless, there are two aspects of this process that refer to the decadence of Greek myths and they, I believe, are the key to understanding the origin of philosophy.

The first aspect refers to the fact that myths do not only naturally evolve, but also are liable to undergo dramatic changes, caused especially by a foreign conquest and a sudden intrusion of a foreign mythology. Such a dramatic change may have occurred between the nineteenth and sixteenth century B.C. when Bronze Age tribes invaded Greece and brought with them a new religion. The early Greek deities were many, immanent and manifest in nature. Nature was the manifestation of the divine. The principal deity was the Mother Goddess or Mother Earth. With the arrival of the invaders, the principal deity becomes the god-man Zeus. In archaic societies every significant action, including war, has a precedence in a mythical, exemplary model, and consequently takes place in the sacred time.[11] Zeus personifies and sets a precedence for the king of an ancient community, a just and wise ruler. In fact, as long the king rules in conformity with Nature, he is the Divine King, the mighty, revered guardian of harmony and order. Nature is still revered. The Divine King protects life. He marries the Mother Goddess of the local community. But with social development, which makes the communities larger, more self-sufficient and independent, the king becomes the symbol of might that can overcome the powers of nature. In the mythical war between the capricious forces of nature symbolized by Titans and the gods under the leadership of Zeus, the god-man is the winner. Consequently, it is he rather than nature who becomes feared and revered. The profane, factual acts thus gain the upper hand over the exemplary and mythical. The separation between the human being and "thou" begins. The Greek myths show that the original relationship of devotional engagement between humans and the "thou," which is the foundation of mythical attitude, is, by the time of Homer and Hesiod, already seriously weakened.

In a mythical society there are two kinds of events that take place in time.[12] First are those that can be called sacred and take place in a sacred time because they find their validation or confirmation in myths. The second are those that follow no exemplary pattern and can be called profane. One of the most important functions of myth is to provide exemplary models for all significant human actions, to validate customs and institutions. However, in Greece in the sixth century B.C., when western philosophy is born, myth can no longer satisfactorily perform this function. Once the separation between humans and the "thou" is initiated, the volitional, aesthetic, and other profane elements enter into myth. This in fact happens to the Greek mythology largely because of Homer and Hesiod. The classical mythology of Homer and Hesiod represents the triumph of the literary work against myth. The gods whom both Homer and Hesiod describe are not only divine, but also show their undisguised human faces. They are moved by passions and commit abuses. When Xenophanes and later Plato accuse these great poets of attributing to the gods all the things that are shameful, they address an audience that is already convinced. These ancient critics of classical mythology do not argue against religion or myth as such, but in the name of a higher idea of the divine they attack the shameful behavior of the gods as depicted by the poets. To sum up, the second important aspect of the process by which myth gave way to philosophy is the fact that Greek myths gradually lost their function as exemplary models for human actions and afflicted Greece with a religious and moral vacuum.

The Beginning of Philosophy. Many scholars perceive, perhaps rightly, something unique in the development of Greek philosophy. It is a widely spread opinion that Thales and his successors ask general questions about the world and propose general, rational answers that are no longer based on theological considerations. The Presocratic thinkers are believed to be not only the first philosophers, but also the first empirical scientists.[13] For Husserl, the rationality and generality of both their questions and answers is a sign of a theoretical attitude, which is the basis of science and which can be sharply contrasted with a practical attitude that refers to myth.[14] It is not my purpose to argue that some of these views may be misleading. In his book on *The Nature of Greek Myths*, Kirk shows that Thales, Anaximenes, and Anaximander continued to be strongly affected by mythical preconceptions, and their cosmologies were based on the theogonical models provided by myths.[15] My fundamental claim is that the way of inquiry that philosophy initiates is primarily the consequence of the decadence of Greek myths. In the initial stage of the development of philosophy, at least some philosophers try to make up for the loss that the corruption of myths brings about. From this point of view, there is no radical break in continuity between myth and philosophy.

By the time of the first philosophers, Greek myths, corrupted by the poets, do not longer provide humans with exemplary models for right conduct. They become bad stories. For Xenophanes, Heraclitus, and Plato, and other Greek philosophers, the classical myth no longer performs its function, but becomes a source of confusion. We can find a striking confirmation of this statement in books II and III of the *Republic* where Plato openly criticizes Homer and Hesiod for teaching falsehoods and for giving bad images of what gods and heroes are like. The gods and heroes of Hesiod and Homer can no longer supply men and women with models for their behavior. The human being loses his devotional engagement with the world. Instead of following the ways prescribed by myth, men and women now choose poets and humans to be their teachers. Unable to undergo a deeper mystical experience, they are now deceived by appearances, the visible things. Heraclitus says:

> For what thought or understanding have they? They follow the poets and take the crowd as their teachers, knowing that there are many bad and few good (fragment 104). Men are deceived over the recognition of visible things, in the same way as Homer, who was the wisest of all the Hellenes (fragment. 56). Homer deserves to be turned out of the lists and whipped. (fragment 43).

For the human being who loses his devotional engagement with the world, the original cosmological representation of myth becomes gradually invalid. He "objectively" disproves the existence of the "thou." He may still listen to myths, but for aesthetic or literary reasons. He becomes indifferent to Nature, and regards everything merely as an object of either his inquiry or exploitation. He becomes a self-seeking individual. When looking at the sea, he does not perceive Poseidon or his horses. Myth becomes a foolish fantasy and is no longer valid for him.

The first Greek philosophers attempt to prevent their

contemporaries from losing their engagement with the world. Their contemporaries lose their devotional engagement because of the corruption of the classical myth. Therefore, philosophy needs to replace myth in ancient Greece. Its function at the early stage is still similar to that of myth. By providing a representation of reality, philosophy reveals the meaning of the whole and directs human behavior. For the Milesians, the world is still alive and divine; it is a "thou." For Thales water is *arche*, the unity and the origin of the living presence. Water makes things grow. It supports the growth and unceasing process of life. Anaximenes says that the original element, *arche*, is not water, but air. It is clear that he does not consider air merely as physical matter. Rather, for him air is also connected with the maintenance of life. It is an agent of vitality. Anaximander objected to the idea of a single, determinate constituent of our world being the original element. He is apparently the least understood among the Milesians. Anaximander declares *arche* to be *apeirion* (something indeterminate, inexhaustible, and indefinite). What he appears to say is that our beginning and end are not known to us. Anaximander reflects upon the very fact of human-being-in-the-world. We rise from chaos and go back to chaos. What is between is cosmos, the precious life. Further, Anaximander expresses the idea of a righteous universe when he says that things "pay penalty and retribution to each other for the injustice according to the assessment of time" (fragment 1). Nature for him is not only alive, but like a person, it is moral and subjected to moral laws.

If we define scientists as those who attempt to describe the world "objectively" in terms of abstract principles and explain it by general laws, Milesians were certainly not scientists. For them the world is alive and divine, it is "thou." They inquire into the world as a whole, and desire to know the whole, but such a knowledge postulates an engagement with the whole and not an "objective," theoretical description. The engagement of the Milesians, and also of subsequent philosophers, including Plato and Aristotle, can be traced to the etymology of the word "philosophy" itself. In the proper sense of this word, "philosophy," "love of wisdom" presupposes being engaged, the attitude of a lover, and not being indifferent. The philosophical attitude of first philosophers is thus still engagement. By contrast to mythological attitude it is not devotional, but rather affective engagement. The stress is no longer put on the supernatural, but rather on the pursuit of the knowledge of the whole and on understanding. It is true that by interpreting them in terms of his theory of four causes, already Aristotle misrepresents the cosmological representations of the Milesians. Further misinterpretations are obvious if we notice the word *phusis* (Nature) is often translated as "the real constitution" and the word *arche* by such terms as "substance" or "principle." But the Milesians are first philosophers, the lovers; they are not empirical scientists.

Objectivity and the Scientific Attitude. For the modern man of science, the phenomenal world is primarily an "It," an object of observation and experiment. According to a perhaps naive, but still prevailing positivistic account of science, science is objective.[16] It derives its objectivity from the objectivity of observation. The way in which scientists look at the world is sometimes described as "scientific attitude." In order to be objective observers, scientists must be indifferent, disinterested, neutral, and impartial.[17] Personal opinions or preferences have to be suspended. No subjective elements are allowed to intrude. Further, the objectivity of observation is the basis of science's reliability. Science is believed to be reliable if it is based on objective, observational statements that can then be transmitted into laws and theories.

One of the key characteristics of modern science is objectivity. Objective, scientific knowledge is held to be independent of the human mind that either creates or understands it. But just as scientific knowledge, derived from observation, presupposes the scientific attitude of being an indifferent observer, so also its verification and sharing with other members of the scientific community requires the same attitude. Without this attitude science would neither be objective nor inter-subjective. Objectivity and scientific attitude are thus interrelated. If this, however, is truly the case, objective knowledge is not independent of the human mind as it is commonly believed. It is dependent upon the states of mind that constitute scientific attitude: on being indifferent, disinterested, neutral and impartial. While defending objectivity in science Karl Popper says:

> My . . . thesis involves the existence of two different senses of knowledge or of thought: (1) knowledge or thought in the subjective sense, consisting of a state of mind or of consciousness or a disposition to behave or to act, and (2) knowledge or thought in an objective sense, consisting of problems, theories, and arguments as such.[18]

Popper radically distinguishes "objective" theories, problems, and arguments from "subjective" states of mind. But once we comprehend that objectivity in science presupposes scientific attitude as its foundation, we can no longer accept that objective scientific knowledge is free from subjectivity. Objective theory is not independent of the human mind.

Being indifferent, disinterested, neutral, and impartial can be contrasted with being engaged. The scientific attitude of a modern empirical scientist lies thus in direct opposition to the mythological attitude, and also to the philosophical attitude, if we understand philosophy traditionally as the love of wisdom. If the scientific attitude seems emotionally neutral, both the mythological and philosophical attitudes are based on feelings, whether those are feelings of devotion, compassion, or the love of humanity and alive nature. But indifference, a lack of feeling, is a state of mind as well. There is subjectivity in scientific objectivity, namely, indifference.

Science looks at the world "objectively," indifferently as if it were an object, but in fact the world is not that. To look at the world as an object is a way of relating to it from a certain perspective and can in fact bring about only its abstraction. This is not the way to know the world as a whole. Science replaces "thou," the life presence, with the dead world of abstracted objects.

Philosophy Rediscovered. The fact that there is a continuity between myth and philosophy that makes early philosophy look more similar to myth than to modern science does not mean that there are not significant differences between myth and philosophy. I wish to explore two distinctions that I believe to be fundamental. First, myth is a wholeness disclosing the world in its completeness. It signifies wisdom, the knowledge of the whole. But, already at its early stage, instead of being wisdom, philosophy is rather a pursuit of wisdom, the desire to arrive at the ultimate knowledge of everything, at the knowledge of the whole. Second, mythical attitude presupposes engagement with the world as a whole of which myth is itself a part. The cosmological representation in myth is founded on devotional engagement. "Objectively" taken, myth may be seen as a foolish or fantastic story, but thus rationalized it does not lead us to the knowledge of the whole. It does not reveal the levels or layers of meanings that can be discovered in it. But a system of philosophy is founded on affective rather than devotional engagement. It can be taken as on object of an examination. This happens in fact already at the beginning of philosophy. Anaximenes says that *arche* is not water but air. Thus, he is certainly not devotionally engaged with Thales' system. Early philosophy appears to have almost the same function as myth: philosophy reveals the meaning of the whole and directs human behavior. Yet, it is also already essentially different from myth. It does not claim the knowledge of the whole and does not posit devotional engagement toward itself.

Myth is a wholeness attuned to the world as a whole because those who live in myth and are guided by it are engaged on many different planes with the whole of which the myth is an integral part. By teaching humans and by regulating the way of their living in devotional engagement with the whole and by gradually disclosing many layers of its meaning, myth reveals the knowledge of the whole. But the knowledge of the whole is not merely theoretical. It is not merely a partial, intellectual knowledge. It embraces the whole of life. Myth reveals the knowledge for which philosophy in a proper sense looks. But it does not disclose this knowledge without appropriate devotional engagement. Myth is completed already at the beginning, whereas philosophy seeks to be completed at the end. Mythical societies live in eternity rather than in historical time. The societies in which philosophy or science plays an important part constantly seek their completion and are in a permanent dissatisfaction with the results of their findings. They live in history and are time oriented. Myth corresponds to eternity, philosophy to the discovery of history.

If myth is taken "objectively" its cosmological representation may no longer make any sense. If a philosophy is subjected to an objective examination, it may perhaps be rejected, but it does not become senseless. The fact that philosophy may be objectively examined and therefore challenged contributes to both its development and decline. On the one hand, it develops into a rich conceptual and intellectual framework as a result of a great debate between contending world views, different schools and philosophical systems that has taken place in the history of philosophy. On the other hand, it declines because it finally ceases to be pursuit of wisdom and largely dissolves into sciences. The scientific paradigm, especially the positivistic one, transforms philosophy. It reduces philosophy to an exercise in language analysis, and deprives the rest of it of the right to exist. It also reduces the human being to a self-interested, self-seeking and thus rationalized individual, moved solely by his passions. Philosophy loses its original sense and, like science, becomes partial knowledge of a part. But I shall not immerse myself any further in the issue of the decadence of philosophy. I wish now to show how philosophy already at its beginning was doomed to decline, and how to regain the love of wisdom.

Philosophy defined as pursuit of wisdom can be understood as the desire to arrive at ultimate knowledge – the knowledge of the whole, but it neither is the knowledge of the whole nor does it posit devotional engagement toward itself. It can be subjected to a critical, objective, or even unsympathetic examination. Hence, there is a lack of consequence in and a danger to philosophy as such: philosophy is the love of wisdom, which presupposes affective engagement with the world, but it may be rejected by an indifferent or cynic sophist. In the long run, philosophy, which in its original form tries to make up for the loss that the corruption of myths brings about, had no chance of survival, like myth. In order to persevere, it had to develop two survival techniques. First, in philosophers like Heraclitus, Plato, Hegel, and Heidegger, it developed highly ambiguous language and non-penetrable esoteric content. Second, in philosophers like Aristotle, Descartes, Kant, and Husserl it aimed at becoming scientific and thus at establishing an unshaken ground on which it could protect itself from possible criticism. In both cases the goal was the same: defense against the profane. When we carefully examine the basic ideas of some highly sophisticated and publicly admired philosophical writings, we can often discover their poverty. The form overcomes the actual content. When we carefully examine some simple myths of so called primitive people, with great surprise we can discover ideas of key importance to our lives. The content overcomes the form.

I would say that the contemporary esoteric stream in philosophy, even if it still inspires many doctoral and master's theses, has become today very problematic, especially in its post-modern version;

whereas the scientific stream has contributed considerably to the decline of original philosophizing, especially in its positivistic and analytic versions. In the proper sense, philosophy is the love of wisdom; pursuit of the knowledge of the whole. But when it turns to be scientific and attempts to look at the world "objectively," that is, as if it were an object, it arrives only at the partial knowledge of a part. What remains largely unquestioned in modern science is its essence. The essence of scientific outlook is indifference. Science regards the world indifferently as an object of scientific research. Consequently, philosophy needs to follow its own path. Philosophy should not look at things as if they were just objects. It needs to recognize the illusion that the partial knowledge brings about. In the proper sense, philosophy as the love of wisdom presupposes being engaged with the world and not being indifferent.

This essay is not intended to provide easy answers to problems that are immense. Even if we do like to think about this, we are probably all aware of our present human condition. As in the Greece of Xenophanes, Heraclitus, and Plato there are still temples, but merely as something that reminds us of the past. Corrupted and weakened religion does not teach today's men and women to live in engagement with the world. Human vices and wicked ideas take the place of gods and become prized. For this reason philosophy arises: to reveal the meaning of the whole, to direct human behavior, and ultimately to prevent humans from destruction. But it fails. Perhaps it is true that it is "too late for God and too early for being." Perhaps it is now either too late or too early to ask God to save us. Perhaps we can once more try the way of original philosophy that is the love of wisdom. But in such a case we have to avoid our old mistake. To place the world before us as an object of indifferent investigation can lead the world to be known only as an abstracted object and not as a whole. Under the surface of illusion that results from such investigation there is a universal knowledge that arises from our devotional and affective engagement with the world.[19]

NOTES

1. G. S. Kirk, *The Nature of Greek Myths* (London: Penguin Books, 1974), p. 38.
2. H. and H. A. Frankfort, *The Intellectual Adventure of Ancient Man* (Chicago: Chicago University Press, 1967), p. 4.
3. Ibid., p. 6.
4. Faith as a unique means of salvation which we can find in Judaism and Christianity is not the devotional engagement that refers to mythological societies. See Mircea Eliade, *Myths, Dreams and Mysteries* (New York: Harper&Row, 1967), pp. 29ff.
5. Ibid., p. 15.
6. Ibid., pp. 95ff.
7. Mircea Eliade, *Patterns in Comparative Religion* (Cleveland: Merdian Books, 1963), p. 426.
8. Kirk, *The Nature of Greek Myths*, p. 60.
9. Ibid., pp. 286f.
10. Ibid., p. 293.
11. Eliade, *Myths, Dreams and Mysteries*, p. 37.
12. Ibid., p. 44.
13. Jonathan Barnes, *The Presocratic Philosophers*, Vol. 1 (London: Routledge, 1979), p. 4.
14. See Edmund Husserl, "The Vienna Lecture" in *The Crisis of European Sciences and Transcendental Philosophy*, trans. by David Carr (Evanston, Ill: Northwestern University Press, 1970), pp. 280–82.
15. Kirk, pp. 295-300.
16. For a naive view of empirical science see A. F. Chalmers, *What Is This Thing Called Science?* (St. Lucia, Qld.: University of Queensland Press, 1976), pp. 1–11.

17. See W. Lawrence Neuman, *Social Research Methods: Qualitative and Quantitative Approaches*, 5th ed. (Boston: Allyn and Bacon, 2003), p. 10.
18. Karl R. Popper, *Objective Knowledge* (Oxford: Oxford University Press, 1979), pp. 108–09.
19. This text was originally published under the title "Rethinking Philosophy: A Reflection on Philosophy, Myth, and Science," *Philosophy Today*, 46.2 (2002), pp. 209-217.

4. Knowing Beyond Science

The only way to full knowledge lies in the act of love.

– Eric Fromm

One of the key characteristics of modern science is objectivity. Scientific knowledge is held to be independent of attitudes, beliefs, and other subjective states of mind of individual scientists. However, just as scientific knowledge, derived from observation, presupposes the "scientific attitude" of being a detached, objective observer, so also its verification and sharing with other members of the scientific community requires the same attitude. Without this attitude, science would neither be objective nor inter-subjective.[1] Objectivity and "scientific attitude" are thus interrelated. If this is the case, objective scientific knowledge is not independent of the human mind as is commonly believed. It is dependent upon the states of mind that constitute scientific attitude: on being indifferent, disinterested, neutral and impartial.

Being a disinterested, objective observer can be contrasted

with being engaged. Once we engage in something, we are no longer indifferent or neutral. We take a personal stand on something. Taking a stand on different issues, holding beliefs, being emotionally and personally involved in many life situations are all characteristic of everyday life. Scientific attitude, which can best be described by the words "neutrality" or "indifference," thus lies in direct opposition to the everyday human attitude based on preferences and feelings. But indifference, a lack of feeling, is a state of mind as well. Once we comprehend that objectivity in science presupposes scientific attitude as its foundation, we can no longer accept the view that objective scientific knowledge is free from subjectivity. There is subjectivity in scientific objectivity, namely, indifference.

Looking at the world indifferently as if it were an object, which is the view of a detached, objective observer, is a way of relating to it from a certain perspective. The pursuit of objectivity leads to abstraction from the individual scientist's personal position in the world. Thomas Nagel goes so far as to assert that "objectivity involves not only a departure from one's individual viewpoint, but also as far as possible, departure from specifically human or even mammalian viewpoint"[2] and allows us to look at the world "not from a place within it, but from nowhere in particular".[3] The move toward objectivity, he claims, reveals what things as they are in themselves, and not as they appear to be. Objective knowledge, thus obtained, is a true account of the actual world. Is this view justified?

Firstly, one can make an objection and argue that there is no knowledge without the knower. The "view from nowhere" must always be a view from somewhere.[4] An individual scientist can abstract from his or her position in the world, his or her preferences and feelings, but cannot go beyond his or her subjectivity in the form of scientific attitude. A complete abstraction from human personality so as to transcend subjectivity and a specifically human or even mammalian viewpoint cannot be conceived of and hence is impossible.

The form of subjectivity that refers to scientific attitude has been described by the word "indifference." Empirical scientists look at the world "objectively," indifferently, as if it were an object. Ideally speaking, they do not enter into personal relationships with the objects of their inquiry. Yet, as I will argue further, by looking at the world in this way, one can learn about them only from a certain viewpoint. An objective account will omit something.[5] Therefore, scientific knowledge can give us only a partial and not a complete picture of the actual world. Moreover, if objective, scientific knowledge is a partial one, it cannot claim to reveal what things are like in themselves. It cannot know things as they are themselves, but only as objects.

Our knowledge is not independent from our state of mind. Objective knowledge is impossible without the scientific attitude of being a detached, neutral observer. The basic emotional states of mind are indifference, love and hate. Indifference can be defined as suspension of feeling, or a lack of feeling towards something. It is the form of subjectivity that is necessary condition for a disinterested process of inquiry and objective knowledge. By contrast, love and hate are two opposing feelings, expressing respectively inclination and disinclination towards something. I shall now analyze the influence of these on our knowledge.

The most striking example of hate can be found in the situation of war. In war, both sides, driven by antagonistic interests, do violence to each other. This gives rise to the passion of hatred: disinclination towards the other side. If I am disinclined towards something, I do not wish to have anything to do with it, and particularly, to know it as it is. Hence, hate does not result in knowledge. It produces and reinforces prejudices that disfigure facts and contribute to false beliefs. To be sure, in the situation of war we can also find some objective knowledge that is instrumental in the destruction of the enemy. Soldiers, trained into instruments of war, may learn how to destroy their enemies effectively. They are not interested in them as persons, but as objects of possible annihilation. In short, indifference may give rise to objective knowledge that is a partial knowledge, but hatred does not give rise to any knowledge at all.

If hate results in separation in strife, love brings about unity. Perhaps the simplest example of love can be found in motherhood. The way in which a loving mother knows her child goes beyond knowing objective properties such as the child's weight or height. Taking care of the child's growth, she cherishes the way in which the child speaks, smiles, walks. Her knowledge requires constant learning: how to respond to and act towards her child in diverse situations. It cannot be reduced to simple, observational propositions. Now, could it be that what the mother knows is unjustified? Is her knowledge nothing more but a collection of illusions, prejudices, emotions and preferences? Can we truly know a person in any other way than as an object or a collection of facts?

How is it possible to know another person? Positivistic epistemology, which is dominant in today's social sciences, denies that we can know another person in a different way than as a physical object. Human beings are assumed to be egoistic, self-interested, pleasure-seeking, rational individuals.[6] We can learn about them only by observing their behavior. What happens in their minds is neither publicly available nor even considered important.

The basic assumption that underlies the epistemology of positivist social science can be traced to the thesis of physicalism. In the words of A.J. Ayer, the thesis is that "to say anything about a person's thoughts, or feelings, or sensations, or private experiences of any kind, is always equivalent to saying something about his physical conditions or behavior".[7] The ground for this thesis is the belief in the privacy of experience. Mental states, such as our thoughts, feelings, or sensations are considered private. They are things to which we alone have access. The possibility of their communication is denied. By contrast, physical objects: material things and their behavior, belong to the public world. They are held to be public because of conjecture that different people can perceive them in a like manner. Consequently, only observational statements, statements about physical objects, can be verifiable and produce knowledge. Knowledge is observational. Thus, according to the positivistic view, when we speak about our mental states, we can refer to our own experiences; but when we speak about the mental states of others, we can refer only to other persons' observational behavior which corresponds to their mental states.[8] Our talk about minds is translated into talk about bodies.

There is, however, a difficulty with the belief in the privacy of experience which supports the thesis of physicalism. It is inconsistent with everyday practice. Firstly, as a matter of fact both in science and in everyday discourse we communicate our thoughts to others. It is difficult to imagine how, without communication of thoughts and ideas, there could be accumulation of knowledge, and how education and science could be possible. Further, we can communicate not only our thoughts to others, but also our attitudes and feelings. If scientific attitude, based on indifference, is a part of proper scholarly conduct and is learned and internalized during many years of schooling,[9] it is because it can be communicated and plays a vital role in scientific activity. It must be shared by scientists to ensure the objectivity and inter-subjectivity of research.

If thoughts and feelings are declared incommunicable, then we can know other persons only as physical objects, by observing them. However, even if, as Ayer maintains, "different people can share the same thoughts and feelings, but they are not literally the same,"[10] and thus a possibility for misunderstanding is open, it does not mean that communication between humans is impossible. Hence, as I will show below, the distinction between private experiences and public objects is ill founded. The objective limitation set on the knowledge of other persons must be declared erroneous.

Our inability to have direct access to the thoughts and feelings of others stems from our being separated individuals. Our separation imparts also our ability to communicate with other people. Speaking about communication, there is always a question as to whether or not the words that we use to describe our private experiences have the same meaning for us and for others. Ayer claims that there is no possible adjustment of our situation as humans by which our separateness could be overcome.[11]

It is true that from the point of view of our bodies, we are distinct, separated individuals. As a physical object, one is clearly not somebody else. But it is not so obvious that we are always separated with respect to our minds. Our mental separateness is a dynamic process. Sharing the same vocabulary and the same values connects people more closely to one another, and makes them less separated in their minds. On the other hand, antagonistic interests and hatred divide people and set them apart. Even some strictly private experiences like our childhood memories, dreams, or concerns can either be shared with other persons of our choice, eventually thus creating a mutual understanding and a sense of emotional unity, or be kept secret.

In each human being there is a deeply rooted need to overcome his or her separateness from others.[12] We fulfill this need in various ways when we seek the attention, acceptance or admiration of others. But the real adjustment of our situation as humans by which separateness is overcome is love. It is the feeling that brings us together. Further, as I will attempt now to show, just like objective scientific knowledge presupposes a scientific attitude, so non-objective but inter-subjective moral knowledge needs a loving attitude as its foundation.

Let us consider a moral statement: "Killing innocent civilians is wrong."[13] Such a statement would probably be true for most rational beings, but not for everyone, as examples taken from wars can show. It is neither tautological, true solely because of the meaning of its terms, nor empirical because it does not make an assertion about any physical object and cannot be verifiable by sense-experience. Since, in light of positivistic epistemology, statements have meanings only if they are either tautological or empirically verifiable, it follows that the statement "Killing innocent civilians is wrong" is meaningless.[14] Still, is this correct? Is the statement "Killing innocent civilians is wrong" merely an expression of feelings and preferences and not a truthful norm based on knowledge? We know that something is the case if we have reasons believe that it cannot be otherwise. What are the possible reasons to believe that the statement, "Killing innocent civilians is wrong," is true; whereas its opposite, "Killing innocent civilians is right," is false?

Most of us have never seen face-to-face the actual killing of civilians. However, once we accept that human experiences are not incommunicable, we can understand the meaning of the phrase "killing innocent civilians." It refers to depriving of life and often subjecting to extreme suffering people who are not legitimate military targets, who, being neither combatants nor criminals, are not guilty of anything. Killing innocent civilians is a crime committed in war.[15] If this is so, killing innocent civilians must surely be wrong. Yet, how do we know this? Instances of such a crime still occur. As some people say, in war anything goes. The killing of civilians is explained by the circumstances of war in which the opposing sides, moved by their own interests and zeal for victory, are impatient with all restraint. There are thus individuals who believe that killing innocent civilians is right. Why are they wrong?

There are disagreements about moral issues. For people who hate others or are indifferent towards them, a moral norm that obstructs the pursuit their interests cannot possibly be anything more than mere words. It will refers to no experiences which they can assimilate as their own and to no value that they can share with others. What is fundamental to an agreement in the realm of both facts and morals is a commonly shared attitude that determines human relatedness to the world. My claim is that in science it is the scientific attitude of being an objective, detached observer, but in ethics it is the loving attitude, the attitude of affective engagement. Without this attitude rational consensus in morals is impossible.

The moral statement, "Killing innocent civilians is wrong," is neither a tautology nor an empirical statement. However, the statement is not just a meaningless expression of feelings. It is not factually, but morally meaningful. Its meaningfulness does not depend upon verifiable facts, but upon its being a true norm which all rational beings whose attitude is love will accept. This statement is both meaningful and true because, once we understand, in the context of reciprocal communication of our experiences, what killing innocent civilians means and what it implies, we can say with full conviction that it is morally wrong and it can never be right.

"The only way to full knowledge lies in the act of love".[16] But what kind of status does such a moral knowledge have? Once we accept that our experiences, thoughts and feelings, are not incommunicable, we can arrive at inter-subjective and non-objective knowledge which is derived from a rational consensus between individuals who exchange, share and debate their experiences; who can say, "we know that something is the case and have good reasons to be sure." There is thus a moral universal knowledge which goes beyond scientific objectivity: knowledge which results from our recognition of others as persons and our affective engagement with the world.[17]

NOTES

1. The way in which empirical scientists look at the world is sometimes described as "scientific attitude." In order to be objective observers, they must be disinterested, neutral, and impartial.

2. Thomas Nagel, "Subjective and Objective" in *Post-Analytic Philosophy* (New York: Columbia University Press, 1985), p. 42.
3. Ibid., p. 41.
4. The phrase "view from nowhere" alludes to Thomas Nagel's book, *The View from Nowhere* (Oxford: Oxford University Press, 1986). It was coined by Lorraine Code to describe the epistemological position of a detached observer. See Lorraine Code, *Rhetorical Spaces* (New York: Routledge, 1995).
5. Nagel, "Subjective and Objective," in *Post-Analytic Philosophy*, p. 45. Nagel notices that the pursuit of objectivity is not an effective method of reaching truth about everything, but he does not draw from his good point appropriate consequences.
6. See W. Lawrence Neuman, *Social Research Methods: Qualitative and Quantitative Approaches*, p. 72.
7. A. J. Ayer, *The Problem of Knowledge* (New York: Penguin, 1984), p. 210.
8. Ibid, p. 215.
9. Neuman, p. 9.
10. Ayer, p. 199.
11. Ibid, p. 217.
12. Erich Fromm, *The Art of Loving* (New York, Harper & Row, 1974), p. 8.
13. Ayer's example of a moral statement was: "Stealing is wrong." I believe that my statement provides a more clear case of a moral norm.
14. This is exactly what Ayer asserted about his "Stealing is wrong."
15. The deliberate killing of civilians is crime and military commanders who order, encourage or tolerate such murder

are fully responsible for it. They must take steps to avoid and limit even unintended civilian deaths. But in war killing innocent civilians may sometimes be unavoidable. See Michael Walzer, *Just and Unjust Wars* (New York: Basic Books, 1977), pp. 316-325.

16. Fromm, p. 26.
17. This is a revised text of my article entitled "Knowing Beyond Science: What Can We Know and How Can We Know?", *Humanitas*, 15.2 (2002), pp. 60-73.

5. Democracy and Politics of the Soul

> I think our city, if indeed it has been completely founded, is completely good . . .
> Clearly, then it will be wise, courageous, moderate, and just.
> — *Plato*

It is generally believed today that democracy, "government of the people by the people and for the people," is the best and only fully justifiable political system. The distinct features of democracy are freedom and equality. Democracy can be described as the rule of the free people who govern themselves, either directly or though their representatives, in their own interest. Why does Plato not consider democracy the best form of government? In the *Republic* he criticizes the direct and unchecked democracy of his time precisely because of its leading features (557a-564a).[1] Firstly, although freedom is for Plato a true value, democracy involves the danger of excessive freedom, of doing as one likes, which leads to anarchy. Secondly, equality, related to the belief that everyone has the right and equal capacity to rule, brings to politics all kinds of power-seeking individuals, motivated by personal gain rather than public good. Democracy is thus highly corruptible. It opens gates to demagogues, potential dictators, and can thus lead to tyranny. Hence, although it may not be applicable to modern liberal democracies, Plato's main charge against the democracy he knows from the ancient Greek political practice is that it is unstable, leading from anarchy to tyranny, and that it lacks leaders with proper skill and morals. Democracy depends on chance and must be mixed with competent leadership (501b). Without able and virtuous leaders, such as Solon or Pericles, who come and go by chance, it is not a good form of government. But even Pericles, who as Socrates says made people "wilder" rather than more virtuous, is considered not to be the best leader (*Gorgias*, 516c). If ruling a state is a craft, indeed statecraft, Plato argues, then politics needs expert rulers, and they cannot come to it merely by accident, but must be carefully selected and prepared in the course of extensive training. Making political decisions requires good judgment. Politics needs competence, at least in the form of today's civil servants. Who then should the experts be and why? Why does Plato in the *Republic* decide to hand the steering wheel of the state to philosophers?

In spite of the idealism with which he is usually associated, Plato is not politically naive. He does not idealize, but is deeply pessimistic about human beings. Most people, living in cities corrupted as they are, are for him fundamentally irrational, driven by their appetites, egoistic passions, and informed by false beliefs. If they choose to be just and obey laws, it is only because they lack the power to act criminally and are afraid of punishment (*Republic*, 359a). Nevertheless, human beings are not vicious by nature. They are social animals, incapable of living alone (369a-b).

Living in communities and exchanging products of their labor is natural for them, so that they have capacities for rationality and goodness. Plato, as later Rousseau, believes that once political society is properly ordered, it can contribute to the restoration of morals. A good political order, good education and upbringing can produce "good natures, and [these] useful natures, who are in turn well educated, [will] grow up even better than their predecessors" (424a). Hence, there are in Plato such elements of the idealistic or liberal world view as the belief in education and progress, and a hope for a better future. The quality of human life can be improved if people learn to be rational and understand that their real interests lie in harmonious cooperation with one another, and not in war or partisan strife. However, unlike Rousseau, Plato does not see the best social and political order in a democratic republic. Opinions overcome truth in everyday life. Peoples' lives and the lives of communities are shaped by the prevailing beliefs. If philosophers are those who can distinguish between true and false beliefs, who love knowledge and are motivated by the common good, and finally if they are not only master-theoreticians, but also master-practitioners who can heal the ills of their society, then they, and not democratically elected representatives, must be chosen as leaders and educators of the political community and guide it to proper ends. They are required to counteract the destabilizing effects of false beliefs on society.

To be sure, Plato's philosophers are not those who can usually be found in departments of philosophy and who are described as the "prisoners who take refuge in a temple" (495a). Initially chosen from among the brightest, most stable, and most courageous children, they go through a sophisticated and prolonged educational training which begins with gymnastics, music and mathematics, and ends with dialectic, military service and practical city management. They have superior theoretical knowledge, including the knowledge of the just, noble, good and advantageous, but are not inferior to others in practical matters as well (484d, 539e). Being in the final stage of their education illuminated by the idea of the good, they are those who can see beyond changing empirical phenomena and reflect on such timeless values as justice, beauty, truth, and moderation (501b, 517b).

If the life of the philosopher-rulers is not of private property, family or wealth, nor even of honor, and if the intellectual life itself seems so attractive, why should they then agree to rule? Plato's answer is in a sense a negative one. Philosophical life, based on contemplative leisure and the pleasure of learning, is indeed better and happier than that of ruling the state (519d). However, the underlying idea is not to make any social class in the city the victorious one and make it thus happy, but "to spread happiness throughout the city by bringing the citizens into harmony with each other ... and by making them share with each other the benefits that each class can confer on the community" (519e). Plato assumes that a city in which the rulers do not govern out of desire for private gain, but are least motivated by personal ambition, is governed in the way which is the finest and freest from civil strife (520d). Philosophers will rule not only because they will be best prepared for this, but also because if they will not, the city will no longer be well governed and may fall prey to economic decline, factionalism, and civil war. Philosophers will approach ruling not as something really enjoyable, but as something necessary (347c-d).

Objections against the government of philosopher-rulers can be made. Firstly, because of the restrictions concerning family and private property, Plato is accused of totalitarianism.[2] However, Plato's political vision differs from a totalitarian state in a number of important aspects. Especially in the *Laws* he make clear that freedom is one of the core values of society (701d). Other values for which Plato stands include justice, friendship, wisdom, courage, and moderation, and not factionalism or terror that can be associated with totalitarian state. Further, the restrictions which he proposes are placed on the governors, rather than on the governed. Secondly, one can argue that there may obviously be a danger in the self-professed claim to rule of the philosophers. Individuals may imagine themselves to be best qualified to govern a country, but in fact they may lose contact with political realities and not be good leaders at all. If philosopher-rulers did not have real knowledge of their city, they would be deprived of the essential credential that is required to make their rule legitimate, namely, that they alone know how best to govern. However, in Plato's view, philosopher-rulers do not derive their authority solely from their expert knowledge, but also from their love of the city as a whole and their impartiality and fairness. Their political authority is not only rational but also substantially moral, based on the consent of the governed. They regard justice as the most important and most essential thing (540e). Even if particular political solutions presented in the *Republic* may be open to questioning, what seems to stand firm is the basic idea that underlies philosophers' governance and that can be traced back to Solon: the idea of fairness based on difference as the basis of the righteous political order. A political order based on fairness leads to friendship and cooperation among different parts of the city.

For Plato, as for Solon, government exists for the benefit of all citizens and all social classes, and must mediate between potentially conflicting interests. Such a mediating force is exercised in the ideal city of the *Republic* by the philosopher-rulers. They are the guarantee of the political order that is encapsulated in the norm that regulates just relations of persons and classes within the city and is expressed by the phrase: "doing one's own work and not meddling with what isn't one's own" (433a-b). If justice is related to equality, the notion of equality is indeed preserved in Plato's view of justice expressed by this norm as the impartial, equal treatment of all citizens and social groups. It is not the case that Plato knew that justice meant equality, but made it inequality as Karl Popper argued. In the ideal city all persons and social groups are given equal opportunities to be happy, i.e. pursue happiness, but not at the expense of others. Their particular individual, group or class happiness is limited by the need of the happiness for all. The happiness of the whole city is not for Plato the happiness of an abstract unity called the *polis*, or the happiness of the greatest number, but the happiness of all citizens that is derived from a peaceful, harmonious, and cooperative union of different social classes. According to the traditional definition of justice by Simonides from Book I, which is reinterpreted in Book IV, as "doing one's own work," each social class receives its proper due in the distribution of benefits and burdens. Social and economic differences, i.e. departures from equality, bring about benefits to people in all social positions, and therefore, are justified. In the Platonic vision of the *Republic*, all social classes get to perform what they are best fitted to do and are unified into a single community by mutual interests. In this sense, although each are different, they are all friends.

It can be contended that the whole argument of the *Republic* is made in response to the denial of justice as a universal moral value expressed in Thrasymachus' statement: "Justice is nothing else than the interest of the stronger" (338c). Moral relativism, the denial of the harmony of interests, and other problems posed by this statement are a real challenge for Plato for whom justice is not merely a notion relative to the existing laws instituted by the victorious factions in power. In the *Laws* a similar statement is made again (714c), and it is interpreted as the right of the strong, the winner in a political battle (715a). By such interpretation, morality is denied and the right to govern, like in the "Melian Dialogue" of Thucydides, is equated simply with might.

The decisions about morals and justice which we make are for Plato "no trifle, but the foremost thing" (714b). The answer to the question of what is right and what is wrong can entirely determine our way of life, as individuals and communities. If Plato's argument about justice presented in both the *Republic* and the *Laws* can be summarized in just one sentence, the sentence will say: "Justice is neither the right of the strong nor the advantage of the stronger, but the right of the *best* and the advantage of the whole community." The best, as explained in the *Republic*, are the expert philosophical rulers. They, the wise and virtuous, free from faction and guided by the idea of the common good, should rule for the common benefit of the whole community, so that the city will not be internally divided by strife, but one in friendship (*Republic*, 462a-b). Then, in the *Laws*, the reign of the best individuals is replaced by the reign of the finest laws instituted by a judicious legislator (715c-d). Throughout this dialogue Plato's guiding principle is that the good society is a harmonious union of different social elements that represent two key values: wisdom and freedom (701d). The best laws assure that all the city's parts: the democratic, the oligarchic, and the aristocratic, are represented in political institutions: the popular Assembly, the elected Council, and the Higher Council, and thus each social class receives its due expression.

Still, a democratic skeptic can feel dissatisfied with Plato's proposal to grant the right to rule to the best, either individuals or laws, even on the basis of tacit consent of the governed.[3] The skeptic may believe that every adult is capable of exercising the power of self-direction, and should be given the opportunity to do so. He will be prepared to pay the costs of eventual mistakes and to endure an occasional civil unrest or even a limited war rather than be directed by anyone who may claim superior wisdom. Why then should Plato's best constitution be preferable to democracy? In order to explain fully the Platonic political vision, the meaning of "the best" should be further clarified.

In the short dialogue *Alcibiades I*, little studied today, though held in great esteem by the Platonists of antiquity, Socrates speaks with Alcibiades.[4] The subject of their conversation is politics. Alcibiades, frequently referred to by Thucydides in the *History of the Peloponnesian War*, the future leader of Athens, highly intelligent and ambitious, largely responsible for the Athenian invasion of Sicily, is at the time of conversation barely twenty years old. The young, handsome, and well-born Alcibiades of the dialogue is about to begin his political career and to address the Assembly for the first time (105a-b). He plans to advise the Athenians on the subject of peace and war, or some other important affair (107d). His ambitions are indeed extraordinary. He does not want just to display his worth before the people of Athens and become their leader, but to rule over Europe and Asia as well (105c). His dreams resemble that of the future Alexander the Great. His claim to rule is that he is the *best*. However, upon Socrates' scrutiny, it becomes apparent that young Alcibiades knows neither what is just, nor what is advantageous, nor what is good, nor what is noble, beyond what he has learned from the crowd (110d-e, 117a). His world-view is based on unexamined opinions. He appears to be the worst type of ignorant who pretends that he knows something but does not. Such ignorance in politics is the cause of mistakes and evils (118a). What is implied in the conversation is that noble birth, beautiful looks, and even intelligence and power, without knowledge, do not give the title to rule. Ignorance, the condition of Alcibiades, is also the condition of the great majority of the people (118b-c).

Nevertheless, Socrates promises to guide Alcibiades, so that he becomes excellent and renowned among the Greeks (124b-c). In the course of further conversation, it turns out that one who is truly the best does not only have knowledge of political things, rather than an opinion about them, but knows one's own self and is a beautiful soul. He or she is perfect in virtue. The riches of the world can be entrusted only to those who "take trouble over" themselves (128d), who look "toward what is divine and bright" (134d), and who following the supreme soul, God, the finest mirror of their own image (133c), strive to be as beautiful and wealthy in their souls as possible (123e, 131d). The best government can be founded only on beautiful and well-ordered souls.

In a few dialogues, such as *Phaedo*, the *Republic*, *Phaedrus*, *Timaeus*, and the *Laws*, Plato introduces his doctrine of the immortality of the soul. His ultimate answer to the question "Who am I?" is not an "egoistic animal" or an "independent variable," as the twentieth century behavioral researcher blatantly might say,[5] but an "immortal soul, corrupted by vice and purified by virtue, of whom the body is only an instrument" (129a-130c). Expert political knowledge for him should include not only knowledge of things out there, but also knowledge of oneself. This is because whoever is ignorant of oneself will also be ignorant of others and of political things, and, therefore, will never be an expert politician (133e). Those who are ignorant will go wrong, moving from one misery to another (134a). For them history will be a tough teacher, but as long they do not recognize themselves and practice virtue, they will learn nothing.

Plato's good society is impossible without transcendence, without a link to the perfect being who is God, the true measure of all things. It is also impossible without an ongoing philosophical reflection on whom we truly are. Therefore, democracy would not be a good form of government for him unless, as it is proposed in the *Laws*, the element of freedom is mixed with the element of wisdom, which includes ultimate knowledge of the self. Unmixed and unchecked democracy, marked by the general permissiveness that spurs vices, makes people impious, and lets them forget about their true self, is only be the second worst in the rank of flawed regimes after tyranny headed by a vicious individual. This does not mean that Plato would support a theocratic government based on shallow religiosity and religious hypocrisy. There is no evidence for this. Freedom of speech, forming opinions and expressing them, which may be denied in theocracy, is a true value for Plato, along with wisdom. It is the basic requirement for philosophy. In shallow religiosity, like in atheism, there is ignorance and no knowledge of the self either. In Book II of the *Republic*, Plato criticizes popular religious beliefs of the Athenians, who under the influence of Homer and Hesiod attribute vices to the gods and heroes (377d-383c). He tries to show that God is the perfect being, the purest and brightest, always the same, immortal and true, to whom we should look in order to know ourselves and become pure and virtuous (585b-e). God, and not human beings, is the measure of political order (*Laws*, 716c).

Plato's critique of democracy may be considered by modern readers as not applicable to liberal democracy today. Liberal democracies are not only founded on considerations of freedom and equality, but also include other elements, such as the rule of law, multiparty systems, periodic elections, and a professional civil service. Organized along the principle of separation of powers, today's Western democracy resembles more a revised version of mixed government, with a degree of moderation and competence, rather than the highly unstable and unchecked Athenian democracy of the fourth and fifth century B.C., in which all governmental policies were directly determined by the often changing moods of the people. However, what still seems to be relevant in Plato's political philosophy is that he reminds us of the moral and spiritual dimension of political life. He provides answers to the questions raised by Thucydides.

Moved by extreme ambitions, the Athenians, like the mythological Atlantians described in the dialogue *Critias*, became infected by "wicked coveting and the pride of power" (121b). Like the drunken Alcibiades from the *Symposium*, who would swap "bronze for gold" and thus prove that he did not understand the Socratic teaching, they chose the "semblance of beauty," the shining appearance of power and material wealth, rather than the "thing itself," the being of perfection (*Symposium*, 218e). "To the seen eye they now began to seem foul, for they were losing the fairest bloom from their precious treasure, but to such who could not see the truly happy life, they would appear fair and blessed" (*Critias*, 121b). They were losing their virtuous souls, their virtue by which they could prove themselves to be worthy of preservation as a great nation.

"Man and city are alike," Plato claims (*Republic*, 577d). Humans without souls are hollow. Cities without virtue are rotten. To those who cannot see clearly they may look glorious but what appears bright is only exterior. To see clearly what is visible, the political world out there, Plato argues, one has first to perceive what is invisible but intelligible, the soul. One has to know oneself. Humans are immortal souls, he claims, and not just independent variables. They are often egoistic, but the divine element in them makes them more than mere animals. Friendship, freedom, justice, wisdom, courage, and moderation are the key values that define a good society based on virtue, which must be guarded against vice, war, and factionalism. To enjoy true happiness, humans must remain virtuous and remember God, the supreme soul and the perfect being.[6]

NOTES

1. My citations come from from Plato. *Republic*. Transl. G. M. A. Grube (revised by C.D.C. Reeve). Indianapolis: Hackett, 1992. I follow a standard form of reference.
2. For the most known critique of "Plato's totalitarianism" see Karl Popper, *The Open Society and Its Enemies*. New York, N.Y.: Harper , 1962. See also Gregory Vlastos, "The Theory of Social Justice in the Polis in Plato's Republic," In *Studies in Greek Philosophy* Vol. 1. Princeton: Princeton University Press, 1993, pp. 69-103.

3. D.D. Raphael, *Problems of Political Philosophy* 2nd ed. London: Macmillan, 1990, p. 83.
4. For an excellent interpretation of this dialogue, see Steven Forde "On the Alcibiades I." In *The Roots of Political Philosophy: The Forgotten Socratic Dialogues*, ed. Thomas L. Pange. Ithaca: Cornell University Press, 1987), pp. 222-39.
5. See Michael P. Sullivan, *International Relations: Theories and Evidences*. Englewood Cliffs, N.J.: Prentice-Hall, 1976, p. 19.
6. This is a revised text of my article entitled "On the Power of Virtue: Universalism of Plato's Political Philosophy," *Dialogue and Universalism*, 13.7-8 (2003), pp. 135-149.

6. Power and Justice in International Reations

Happiness lies in liberty and liberty in valor.

— *Thucydides*

Often regarded as the father of realism in international relations, Thucydides was a historian and an original political thinker who described and analyzed social and political events that occurred during the Peloponnesian War, which broke out in 431 B.C. between Athens and Sparta. Thucydides's masterpiece, the *History of the Peloponnesian War* is not a work of political philosophy nor a sustained theory of international politics. Much of the *History* consists of paired speeches by personages who argue both sides of an issue. In these speeches and in Thucydides' own comments on the events that take place, we can catch a glimpse of a theory that is implied, but nowhere fully formulated or made explicit. Although Thucydides implies that he exemplifies universal truths about human nature, civil society, and interstate relationships, he does not present his point of view explicitly, and never engages with other thinkers in a debate.[1] Nevertheless, if the *History* is described as the only acknowledged classical text in international relations, and if it inspires theorists from Hobbes to contemporary international relations scholars, this is because it is more than a chronicle of events, and a theoretical position can be extrapolated from it.

The *History of the Peloponnesian War* is usually seen as an archetypal statement of power politics. Thucydides is regarded as a political realist who asserts that the pursuit of moral principles does not enter the world of international affairs.[2] I want to show that, on the contrary, we find in Thucydides a complex theory. He supports neither extreme realism, in which international morality is denied, nor utopian idealism that overlooks the aspect of power in international relations. He is profoundly interested in ethical issues in domestic and international politics. Against the provocative title of the recent article of David Welch, "Why International Relations Theorists Should Stop Reading Thucydides,"[3] I argue that both theorists and practitioners of international politics should read Thucydides, and can greatly benefit by reading him.

Thucydides' Realism. The task that Thucydides sets for himself is not just to describe the harsh events that occurred during the Peloponnesian War "and will always happen as long as human nature remains the same" (3.82.2).[4] As he says on its opening pages, the *History* is not a piece of writing designed to meet the taste of the immediate public, but is meant to last forever. He is not merely interested in reconstructing historical events, using the best evidence available, but in providing their general explanation. His work is essentially a study of human and state behavior, in which a theory is implied and permanent characteristics of human affairs and international politics are revealed. Because of his pessimism about human nature, his emphasis on power, and his recognition that morality has little place in inter-state relations, he is often credited with being the first writer in the tradition of political realism.[5]

What is realism? Realism is a view of international politics that stresses its competitive and conflicting side.[6] The principal actors in the international arena are states that are concerned with their own security, act in pursuit of their national interests, and struggle for power. Thucydides seems to subscribe to this view. Distinguishing between immediate and underlying causes of the Peloponnesian War, he does not see its underlying cause in the Athenian intervention in the conflict between Corcyra and Corinth, her siege of Potidaea, or her ban on trade with Megara - the events that occurred immediately before its outbreak. He locates the root of the war in the changing distribution of power between the two blocks of Greek city-states: the Delian League and the Peloponnesian League. According to him, the growth of Athenian power made the Spartans fear for their security, and thus compelled them into war (1.23.6). What he says resonates strongly with realist arguments on how the anarchic structure of the international system affects the behavior of states. The realists find the absence of a ruler, literally *anarchy*, the defining element of international politics and primary determinant of international political outcomes. The lack of a rule-making and enforcing common authority means, they claim, that each state is responsible for its survival and is free to define its own power interests. In the words of the Athenian envoys at Melos, if there is no international government that can enforce order, "the independent states survive [only] when they are powerful" (5.97.2). International anarchy leads thus to the overriding role of power in inter-state relations and causes all states to be motivated by fear and mutual distrust. To attain security, states increase their relative power and engage in power balancing for the purpose of deterring potential aggressors. Wars are fought to prevent any competing nations from becoming militarily stronger.

The negative side of this emphasis on power is the realists' skepticism regarding the applicability of universal ethical norms to relations among states. National politics is the realm of authority and law, whereas international politics, unrestrained by any higher moral laws, is a sphere without justice characterized by active or potential conflict between states. A confirmation of this position can again be found in the "Melian Dialogue" (5.85-113). This dialogue relates to the events of 416 B.C., when Athens invaded the neutral island of Melos. The Athenian envoys present the Melians with a choice between destruction or surrender, and from the outset ask them not to appeal to justice, but to think about their survival. They say: "We both know that the decisions about justice are made in human discussions only when both sides are under equal compulsion, but when one side is stronger, it gets as much as it can, and the weak must accept that" (5.89). To be "under equal compulsion" means to be subjected to a common authority. Since such an authority above states does not exist, the Athenians argue that the only right in the world of anarchy is the right of the stronger to dominate the weaker. They explicitly equate right with might, and exclude considerations of justice from foreign affairs. Further, the right of the stronger to dominate is for them a natural law. "Nature always compels gods (we believe) and men (we are certain) to rule over anyone they can control" (5.105.2). Hence, in the Athenian speech there is implied not only a denial of international morals, but also a certain view of humankind that is essential for the realist view of international politics. International anarchy would not lead to conflict between nations if they were all populated by angels. Whether explicitly, as in classical realism, or implicitly, as in neorealism, the realistic theory premises an egoistic human nature.[7] Human beings are perceived as self-interested and power-seeking, moved by the drive to dominate others, and not influenced by either compassion or any moral rules.

Realism is implied in the statements of the Athenian envoys at Melos and in the way Thucydides explains the cause of the

Peloponnesian War. Moreover, the same outlook of international politics is expressed in the very first speech given by the Athenians in the *History*, namely, at the debate at Sparta, just before the outbreak of the war. The Athenians refer to three motives that have led them to obtain and keep their empire: fear, honor, and self-interest (1.75.3; 1.76.2). A similar motivational triad can be found in Hobbes' *Leviathan* and in twentieth-century realists.[8] Nearly all realists place fear at the core of state motivation. Fear is a defensive motive, based on the desire for self-preservation; however, honor and self-interest, desires for recognition and gain, are fundamentally competitive and acquisitive. These three motives are paralleled in Pericles' "Last Speech" as safety, glory, and wealth (2.63-64). Athenian imperialism is thus justified on the grounds of security concerns, recognition, and expediency, but not on moral grounds. Further, the Athenians affirm the priority of power over justice in international relations and provide justification for this. They argue that morality cannot be put ahead of power because as a rule "the weaker are held by the stronger" (1.76.2). No one who can obtain something by power will be deterred not to use it. To believe otherwise, they suggest, would be to mislead oneself about the nature of international politics.

The Athenians give then strong support to a realist position. The question is, however, to what extent the view of Athenian realism coincides with Thucydides' own viewpoint. Is his realism the same as the realism of the Athenian envoys at Melos and of the Athenians at the debate at Sparta? Is he a realist at all? Thucydides' *History* provides an account of debates between groups and individuals, holding often opposite views. The political discourse that he describes is plural, not single. Although fragments of the "Melian Dialogue" and other parts of the *Peloponnesian War* support a realistic reading, Thucydides' realism cannot be deduced from selected fragments but must be assessed on the basis of the wider context of his book. The "Melian Dialogue" itself provides us with a plurality of contending perspectives.

Realism Versus Idealism in the Melian Dialogue. Political realism is usually contrasted with idealism or liberalism, a theoretical perspective that puts stress on international norms, interdependence between states, and international cooperation.[9] The "Melian Dialogue," which is one of the most frequently commented upon parts of Thucydides' *History*, presents the classic dilemma between idealist and realist thinking: Can international politics be based on a moral order derived from the principles of peace and justice or will it remain the playground of conflicting national interests and power?

For the Melians, who employ idealistic arguments, the choice is between war and subjection (5.86). They do not wish to lose their freedom, and in spite of the fact that they are militarily weaker than the Athenians, they are prepared to defend themselves (5.100; 5.112). They base their arguments on an appeal to justice (5.86), and refuse to concede that justice is a mere matter of expediency, but understand it as a universal moral principle. They associate justice with fairness, and regard the Athenians as unjust (5.90; 5.104). Also, they put their trust in alliances and hope for military assistance from their ally, Sparta. They respect the gods and believe in honor, saying that their weakness will be made up by the aid of the gods supporting their just cause and the help of the Spartans, whom they hold to be honorable (5.104; 5.112). Hence, in the speech of the Melians one can identify such elements of the idealistic or liberal world view as the beliefs that nations have the right to exercise political independence, states have mutual obligations to one another that they will carry out, and a war of aggression is unjust.

The Athenian response is based on such key realist concepts as security and power, and is informed not by what the world should be but what it is. The Athenians urge the Melians to look at the facts, namely to recognize their military inferiority, to consider the potential consequences of their decision, and to think about their own survival (5.87; 5.101). They exclude consideration of justice from their discussion and appeal to the identity of interests. (5.89; 5.91). They are concerned about their security and express fear that the independent Melos may endanger them (5.99). They argue that it will be better for both sides if Melos gives in. The Melians will save themselves from ruin and the Athenians will reap profits from them (5.93). Melos will add to the empire and no longer be a potential security threat (5.97). Furthermore, the Athenians describe the honor and justice of the Spartans, to which the Melians refer, as mere hypocrisy that masks the Spartan interests. Considering the Athenian power and the risk of military action, they claim that it is foolish to believe Sparta will ever come to help and fight for Melos (5.105; 5.109). They advise the Melians not to be distracted by a false notion of honor, which in the absence of strength can only bring them disaster and the dishonor of defeat, or to depend on mere hopes, but to think only about their own country and how to survive in the present circumstances (5.111).

In spite of these realist arguments, the Melians refuse to submit and decide to fight for their independence. After some initial successes on their part, the Athenian siege succeeds. The Melians pay the highest price for their choice. Melian men of military age are killed. Women and children are sold into slavery. Melos loses statehood after seven hundred years of her history. The island is repopulated by Athenian colonists. This tragic story shows that in the end a theory of international relations "involves the ultimate experience of life and death, national existence and national extinction."[10] It is a practical theory, the theory of survival. In the first recorded debate between idealism and realism, realism is the winner, if not by the strength of arguments, then clearly by the force of the Athenian army. There are, nevertheless, reasons to believe that Thucydides does not accept the "radical realism" advocated by the Athenians at Melos. The Athenians do not act as his mouthpiece. Equally, he does not identify his position with the "utopian idealism" represented by the Melians. Both positions reveal serious theoretical weaknesses.

The Melians put high value on courage and honor, and love their country. They have a sense of justice and respect alliances. They are thus in a sense virtuous people. Some of their values resemble those of the Athenians from the earlier period. In one of his speeches, Pericles, the Athenian leader, who dies in the early stage of the War, says that for people who have a choice, to go to war is always a folly. However, when the choice is either to submit to neighbors or to take on dangers to preserve independence, it is better to fight (2.61.1). Contending that not to resist subjugation would be cowardly and shameful, the Melians make the same choice that Pericles suggests and that the Athenians once made themselves when, displaying great courage, they stood alone against the overwhelming might of Persia (1.73-74). The element that they, nevertheless, lack and that does not allow them to be victorious is what Pericles describes as a "strategy based on reality which affords predictable results" (2.62.5). Although they are courageous, the Melians lack resources and foresight. They are guided more by their hopes than by the evidence at hand and prudent calculations. They appeal to justice, which is not listened to, and call for help from outside, which cannot be obtained. Ultimately, they are good and courageous, but politically naive. The kind of utopian idealism that they display leads, because of their lack of good judgment, foresight, and intelligent planning, to martyrdom: the death of combatants and the extreme suffering of civilians, and in the end to the destruction of their political community. Idealism of those who are unable to survive is for Thucydides of no use, and is reported by him solely as a warning against any future political wishful thinking. All the noble aspirations of the Melians are ruined because they do not take into consideration the actual practice of states and do not make provision for their own security.

The Athenians at Melos reveal themselves as models of rational self-interested agents. They use available means to realize the objectives that they set out. There is a seemingly powerful realist logic behind the Athenian arguments. Their position, based on security concerns and expediency, possesses rationality, intelligence, and foresight. However, on close examination their logic contains serious flaws. Melos, a relatively weak state, does not pose any real security threat to them. Their slaughter of the Melians is a tragic error. The destruction of Melos does not change the course of the Peloponnesian War, which is lost by Athens a few years later. The Athenians argue that the international world, imperfect as it is, is ruled by the law that the weaker are dominated by the stronger, and therefore, moral values cannot be applied to it. They do not only acknowledge the lack of justice in interstate relations, but provide justification for this. Consequently, they do not only describe interstate relations, but also prescribe to states the way of domination. Their radical realism is not merely descriptive and defensive, but normative and offensive, and can be better termed as *realpolitik*.[11] On the grounds of the purported lack of universal moral standards in international politics and selfishness of states, the Athenians glorify war and conquest, and act accordingly. They replace moral norms with *raison d'état*, state's expediency, as the highest norm. However, they do not recognize that self-interest and the rules of might alone cannot provide sufficient basis for a practical theory of international politics. In his *History*, Thucydides shows that if it is unrestrained by moderation and a sense of justice, power brings about the uncontrolled desire for more power. There are no logical limits to the size of an empire. Drunk with the prospect of glory and gain after they conquer Melos, the Athenians engage in the war against Sicily. They do not pay attention to the Melian argument that considerations of justice are useful to all in the longer run (5.90). As they overestimate their strength and finally lose the war, the Athenian self-interested logic is indeed very short-sighted.

It is utopian to ignore the selfishness of states and be blind to the reality of power in international relations, but it is equally blind to rely on power alone. Thucydides would support neither naive idealism nor cynical *realpolitik*. If he can still be regarded as a political realist, his realism is neither *realpolitik*, in which international morality is denied, nor neorealism, in which moral questions are largely ignored. His realism is neither immoral nor amoral. In his realism, selfishness is recognized, but is not exalted and presented as a value. Moderation and a sense of justice should keep states from becoming too opportunistic in defining and pursuing their interests. Thucydides' realism can be compared to that of Raymond Aron, Reinhold Niebuhr, and Hans Morgenthau, the twentieth-century classic realists, who, although sensible to the demands of power and national interest, would not deny that political actors on the international scene come under moral judgment.[12] He is profoundly engaged in reflecting on ethical issues in domestic and international politics.

Politics and Ethics. While discussing the violent events that occurred at Corcyra during the civil war (3.82-85), Thucydides attributes the growing wickedness, not only at Corcyra but in the whole Hellenic world, to factionalism and the deterioration of moral uprightness (3.83.1-2). Because it is ridiculed, modesty, the simple virtue found in noble natures, disappears. The excessive desire to rule out of selfishness, greed, and personal ambition prevails (3.82.6). Society becomes divided into two opposing camps. Contending political parties promote their policies under fair-sounding slogans, like "equality for all" or "limited government," pretending thus to serve the public, but in fact they struggle for power without any consideration for justice and the common good (3.82.7). Whatever means to win is used, and both sides commit the most horrible atrocities against one another. People go to every extreme. Oaths are not kept. There is disrespect for piety. Revenge is admired. There is even a revolution in language. Words take on new meanings (3.82.4-5). Acts of thoughtless aggression are described as courageous. Moderation is held to be a cloak for unmanliness. Plotting becomes a justifiable means of defense. Moreover, factionalism turns into the most overwhelming factor. The attributes of being a real man are now partisanship and violent fanaticism. Party membership becomes a stronger tie than that of the family. Those who wish to stay as neutral in the middle are destroyed (3.82.8). No argument is strong enough to convince the sides to terminate their mutual hostility.

The civil war in Corcyra is the paradigm of social disintegration. There are many similarities between the events that take place in Corcyra and the later revolution in Athens that leads to overthrowing democracy and establishing oligarchy (2.65-71). For Thucydides the *polis* is not an abstract entity that has laws of its own. The state cannot be separated from the human beings composing the society. Even if a state can be regarded as a legal abstraction, it is not the state that makes decisions, but individuals. This is why most of Thucydides' ethical words and phrases are used interchangeably to describe individuals and states. His ethical concerns, far from being an expression of abstract thinking, are related to the actual conditions in which states are found. A virtuous political body depends on good qualities of its individual members, and above all on the quality of its leadership. A bad one is corrupted by vice. The disintegration of society that occurs in both Corcyra and Athens is described by such negative ethical words and phrases as injustice, selfishness, greed, disregard for piety, faction, arrogance, envy, revenge, deceit, fear, cowardice, and cruelty.[13] The laudable characteristics of both individual character and a virtuous society, such as respect for law, tolerance, openness, courage, moderation, justice, foresight, self-control, cautious deliberation, prudence, and fraternity, which we can find in Pericles' "Funeral Oration" (ii.35-46), where he describes the Athenian democracy, are absent.

Pericles' Athens stands in Thucydides' *History* for the supreme achievements of civilization: material, political, and ethical. By contrast, Athens of the revolution and the oligarchic rule following it, is a model of political and moral decline. In his famous oration Pericles suggests that the Athenian democracy is a good constitution because it allows the admirable individual and public qualities that he mentions to flourish. He himself displays such prime qualities of character as moderation, foresight, prudence, good judgment, independence of thought and action, and incorruptibility, and it is during his leadership that Athens reaches the peak of its greatness (2.65). Nevertheless, in Pericles' speeches there are also the germs of vice that infect Athens and bring about her downfall. Since it produces immoderate individuals, Thucydides suggests, the excessive love of power in international politics will remove all restraint from domestic politics as well.[14] Pericles inspires Athenian imperial ambitions and appeals to glory, which ultimately leads the Athenians to excess (2.62-64). The ancient modesty or simplicity, which can be associated with a certain sense of limit, disappears not only from the Corcyran, but also from the Athenian character. The successors of Pericles do not follow his cautious and intelligent war policy but manage the state for their private ambition and private gain (2.65.7). They are not, like Pericles, leaders of public opinion, but striving for popularity, they form policies to suit the whims of the people, regardless of whether these policies are actually good for the state (2.65.10). Ultimately this results in a terrible defeat of the Athenians in Sicily and the oligarchic revolution that follows.

The contrast that Thucydides expresses between Pericles and his successors, and between the Athens of Pericles and the Athens of revolution, suggests that material and political achievements of society are inseparable from its morals. Politics is not merely a matter of some structural considerations, but is related to ethics. The state of different communities may range from a supremely civilized community, based on virtue, downwards to a society degraded by vice and torn apart by civil strife.

Thucydides History as "Lasting Possession." Thucydides' *History* was meant by him to be a "lasting possession." It would be erroneous, however, to identify that what he wanted to convey to posterity was a narrow realist theory of international relations. His realism refuses to be confined to the narrow realm of security and power, but takes into account the whole political reality with its ideas, passions, and follies[15] He neither denies international morals nor, like today's neorealists, ignores them in the name of pretended scientific objectivity. On the contrary, in the *Peloponnesian War*, unlike the writings of most of realists, we can find a deep reflection on ethics in its relation to politics. In much the same way as a physician who pronounces his diagnosis, Thucydides examines the causes of political disorder and studies the ways in which ethical characteristics of a state, or their lack, affect its condition.[16] Like other ancient Greek writers before and after him, such as Hesiod, Solon, Aeschylus, as well as Plato and Aristotle, he considers the lack of morals to be a serious disease of the *polis*. In this way he is a part of the Hellenic moral tradition in which Western political philosophy is deeply rooted.

One of the main issues that Thucydides considers is the effect of power when it is not kept within the bounds of moderation and justice in both domestic and international politics. Although he never precisely defines justice, it is clear that this and other ethical concepts are for him neither culturally nor historically relative. The absence of justice as a universal moral value is always lamentable. A society that leaves no room for justice and moderation, that knows no law and no limit, Thucydides concludes, is doomed to fail. Humans are rational actors only in a superficial way. At a deeper level, lacking a sense of justice and moderation, they become fundamentally irrational and their irrationality destroys their understanding of what is expedient for them. They often learn moderation only by defeat. The Athenians finally lose the war because, moved by the love of power alone, they overestimate their strength, develop poor policies, and choose wrong leaders. As numerous other examples from world history can show,[17] no power is ever immune to such miscalculation.[18]

NOTES

1. In his work, which can impress us by its depth and attention to detail, Thucydides discusses a number of topics. G. F. Abbot puts this as follows: "Hardly a problem of statesmanship is left untouched. . . . The advantages of the sea power (I.142, 143; II.62), the weakness inherent in the nature of a coalition (I.141), the respective merits of severity and magnanimity towards rebellious subjects (III.39-40; 44-48), and many other questions of perennial interests are discussed with a perspicacity which has never been excelled." See G. F. Abbot, *Thucydides: A Study in Historical Reality* (New York: Russell&Russell, 1970), pp. 41-42.
2. Realists regard Thucydides as the fonder of realism and their inspiration. In the collected work entitled *Roots of Realism*, Thucydides occupies a prominent place among such realists as Machiavelli, Carr, Niebuhr, and Morgenthau. See Benjamin Frankel, ed. *Roots of Realism* (London: Frank Cass, 1966).
3. See David Welch, "Why International Relations Theorists Should Stop Reading Thucydides," *Review of International Studies*, 29.3 (2003), p. 301-319. Welch does not want us to take the title of his article literally. He is against a strictly realist reading of the Thucydides' work, and argues that we should not read into it our own assumptions and biases, or reduce it to a series of banalities.
4. My citations come from Thucydides, *On Justice, Power and Human Nature: The Essence of Thucydides' History of the*

Peloponnesian War, trans. Paul Woodruff (Indianopolis, Indiana: Hackett). I follow a standard form of reference (book, section, line).

5. For discussions of Thucydides' realism from different perspectives, see Peter J. Ahrensdorf, "Thucydides' Realistic Critique of Realism," *Polity*, 30.2 (1997), pp. 231-65. David Boucher, *Theories of International Relations: From Thucydides to the Present.* (Oxford: Oxford University Press, 1998), pp. 67-89; Michael T. Clark, "Realism Ancient and Modern: Thucydides and International Relations," *Political Science and Politics*, 26.3 (1993), pp. 491-4; Daniel Garst, "Thucydides and Neorealism," *International Studies Quarterly*, 33.1 (1989), pp. 3-27. Michael Doyle, "Thucydidean Realism," *Review of International Studies*, 16.3 (1990), pp. 223-37; Steven Forde, "Varieties of Realism: Thucydides and Machiavelli," *Journal of Politics*, 54.2 (1992), pp. 372-93; Paul A Rahe, "Thucydides' Critique of *Realpolitik*," *Security Studies*, 5 (1995), pp. 105-41.
6. See Jack Donnelly, *Realism and International Relations* (Cambridge: Cambridge University Press, 2000); Robert G. Gilpin, "The Richness of the Tradition of Political Realism," *Neorealism and Its Critics*, ed. Robert O. Keohane (New York: Columbia University Press, 1986), pp. 301-21.
7. See Donnelly, p. 9.
8. Ibid., p. 43.
9. See Micheal W. Doyle, "Liberalism and World Politics," *American Political Science Review*, 80 (1983), pp. 1151-70.
10. Martin Wight, "Why Is There No International Theory?," *International Theory: Critical Investigations*, ed. James Der Derian (London: MacMillan, 1995), p. 33.
11. *Realpolitik* has much in common with the practice of *raison d'état* in the eighteenth century. It denotes politics based on

force, reliance on naked power, ruthlessness and fraud. Moral considerations are excluded for the sake of geopolitical and strategic gain. Power dictates what is just. The term was coined by Ludwig von Rochau in *Gründsatze der Realpolitik* (1853).

12. See Raymond Aron, *Peace and War: A Theory of International Relations*, trans. Richard Howard and Annette Baker Fox (New York: Doubleday, 1966), especially chapter 19; Hans Morgenthau, *Politics among Nations: The Struggle for Power and Peace*. 2nd ed. (New York: Alfred A. Knopf, 1956), chapter 1; Reinhold Niebuhr, *Moral Man and Immoral Society: A Study in Ethics and Politics* (New York: Charles Scribner's Sons, 1932).
13. Mary Frances Williams, *Ethics in Thucydides: The Ancient Simplicity* (Lanham, Md.: University Press of America, 1998), pp. 24-5.
14. See Steven Forde, "Power and Morality in Thucydides," *Thucydides' Theory of International Relations*, ed. Lowell S. Gustafson (Baton Rouge: Louisiana State University Press, 2000), pp. 151-73.
15. Aron, p. 599.
16. Williams, p. 41.
17. Toynbee writes the French "had lent themselves to militarism for 376 years (A.D. 1494-1870), till they had been cured of it by a crushing German resort. A Swedish militarism that had been rampant since Gustavus Adolphus (*regnabat* A.D. 1611-32) had disembarked his expeditionary force on German soil on the 27-28th June 1630, had been extinguished by a subsequent and consequent Swedish experience of being bled white by Charles XII (*regnabat* A.D. 1697-1718). A Spanish militarism that had been coeval with its French counterpart had evaporated after the Thirty Year War. . . .

Spanish, Swedish, French hearts had been changed, sooner or later, by the experience of learning through suffering; and since A.D. 1914 the Germans had received, in their punishment for a repeated sin, a double measure of this sovereign spiritual education." See Arnold J. Toynbee, *A Study of History*, vol. 9 (Oxford: Oxford University Press, 1954), pp. 499-500.

18. This text was originally published under the title "How International Relations Theorists Can Benefit by Reading Thucydides," *The Monist*, 89.2 (April 2006), pp. 231-43.

7. In Defense of International Order

> Among the traits characteristic of human beings is their impending desire for society,
> that is for social life – not of any and every sort, but peaceful and organized.
> – *Grotius*

Hugo Grotius (1583-1645), Huigh de Groot in Dutch, lived during turbulent times in which politics mixed with religion. The emerging sovereign and mutually independent states of Europe were incessantly fighting over territorial, dynastic and commercial matters, as well as over differences in religion. The Thirty Years War, arguably one of the most cruel and lawless wars in European history, broke out in 1618 as a result of religious quarrels. The sovereigns of Grotius's time did not consider themselves bound by international agreements and they were rather unscrupulous in interpreting and applying them. They were thus followers of the doctrine of *raison d'état* and disciples of Niccolò Machiavelli, whose work *The Prince* taught them to break any treaty, when the advantages that had induced them to conclude it ceased to exist.

Machiavelli never used the phrase *ragione di stato* (reason of state) or its French equivalent, *raison d'état.* Nevertheless, the contention that, in order to maintain or protect the state, it is appropriate for a sovereign to engage in a morally reprehensible course of action is central to his political theory. Under his influence, this view of international conduct became the main theme of an entire genre of sixteenth-century Italian political writings, the most notable contribution to which was Giovanni Botero's work *Ragione di Stato.*[1] It was, however, in seventeenth-century France, in the policies of Cardinal Richelieu aimed at the furthering of the Catholic faith and the benefit of the Christian state, and later in Germany, that Machiavellian political ideas came to prominence and contributed to a significant evolution of the doctrine of *raison d'état.* With the breakdown of the unity of western Christendom caused by the Reformation, the rise of the modern state system, and the expanding secularization of European culture, this doctrine lost its preoccupation with any religious ends, and deteriorated into a materialistic ability for calculation of what was necessary for the interest of the state. Frederick the Great (who called Machiavelli the enemy of mankind but closely followed his advice) expressed this doctrine as "princes are slaves to their resources, the interest of the state is their law, and this law is inviolable".[2] *Raison d' état* became the main principle of European interstate relations, and served as a justification of the methods a number of statesmen felt obliged to affirm in their foreign-policy practice.[3] These methods, outlined in *The Prince*, involved conquering either by force or fraud, destroying cities, putting to death anyone who could do harm, moving the inhabitants from one place to another, establishing colonies, replacing old institutions with new ones, and extending the territory and power of the state at the expense of rivals. The question of morality, in the sense of norms restraining states in their mutual relations, either did not arise or was subordinated to the competitive struggle for power.

What ultimately counted for Machiavelli were not moral scruples or norms, but *raison d'état*: whatever is good for the state. Machiavellism has become associated with a certain kind of political behavior in which expediency is placed above morality. This kind of behavior existed long before Machiavelli, and was long before him debated by political philosophers. The arguments of the Athenian envoys presented in the "Melian Dialogue" by Thucydides, of Thrasymachus in Plato's *Republic*, and of Carneades to whom Grotius refers all furnish a great challenge to the classical view of the unity of politics and ethics. However, before Machiavelli, this amoral or immoral stream of thinking had never prevailed over the prevailing political tradition of Western thought. It was only the Machiavellian justification of resorting to evil as a legitimate means of achieving certain political ends that persuaded so many thinkers and political practitioners after him. This justification was further carried on by the theorists of the doctrine of *raison d'état*. The tension between expediency and morality lost its validity in the sphere of politics. The concept of a double morality, private and public, was invented. Ethics was subjected to politics. The good of the state was interpreted as the highest moral value. National power was extended as a nation's right and duty. In the Marxist version of this doctrine, a superior type of morality was assigned to the revolutionary cause. In the name of such a "higher" morality, identified with the interest of the proletariat or of the state, grave crimes against humanity have been committed. Actions which employed violent, cruel, or otherwise customarily immoral means were regarded as legitimate to exigencies of "progressive change."

In this article I present Grotius's argument against *raison d'état* and his defense of the rule of law in international relations. His major work, *De Jure Belli ac Pacis* (*On the Law of War and Peace*), does not contain any reference to the Florentine thinker. Nevertheless, it is principally against Machiavelli that Grotius directs his argument. He challenges the views of adherents of the doctrine of *raison d'état* who give rulers the license to disobey legal and moral norms whenever the vital interests of the state are at stake.

Grotius's Argument against Raison d'État. Drawing our attention to the value of international law, Grotius writes, in the Prolegomena to *De Jure Belli ac Pacis*: "Many hold, in fact, that the standard of justice which they insist upon in the case of individuals within the state is inapplicable to a nation or the ruler of a nation."[4] He tells us that there are those who regard international law with contempt, "as having no reality except an empty name."[5] Such writers consider that for a state nothing is unjust which is expedient and that the conduct of foreign policy cannot be performed without injustice. Powerful states can afford to pursue their policies without regard to law and solely in the light of their own advantage. Grotius rejects these views. In humanist fashion, instead of attacking directly his contemporary opponents, he makes his argument against Carneades (215-129 BC), a natural law critic and a classical representative of the belief that in international politics nothing is unjust which is expedient.

Carneades's position can be summarized as follows. There is no universally valid natural law, discoverable by "right reason," which determines what is right and wrong. Natural law has no basis because all creatures, human beings and animals, are impelled by nature to pursue ends advantageous for themselves.[6] Therefore, nothing is right or just by Nature, and all laws are conventional. Human beings impose them upon themselves for expediency, and such laws vary among different peoples and change at different times. Justice is derived from utility and is based only on calculation of the advantage of living together in a particular society. Such advantage is apparent in the case of citizens who, singly, are powerless to protect themselves. But strong individuals or powerful states, since they contain in themselves all things required for their own protection, do not need justice.[7] They need acknowledge no higher law but their own strength. The notion of justice is thus not applicable to relations between states, or if there is justice, "it is supreme folly, since one does violence to ones own interests if one consults the advantage of others."[8] Carneades, to use the phrase of Reinhold Niebuhr, is in short one "in the long line of moral cynics in the field of international relations" who know no law beyond self-interest.[9]

To Grotius, justice is not folly. He defends natural law as follows. First, he attacks the view that every animal is impelled by nature to seek only its own good. Even animals can restrain their self-serving appetites, to the advantage of other animals, most obviously their offspring.[10] Sheep-dogs, for example, go in advance of their flocks, fighting till death, if necessary, to protect the flocks and shepherds from hurt. If this is the case with animals, it is even more so with humans, who are rational creatures. Humans can benefit not only themselves, but also others by the ability to recognize others' needs. They can refrain, even with inconvenience to themselves, from doing hurt.[11] They have been endowed with the faculty of knowing good and evil, and of acting according to general principles. What is characteristic of human beings is "an overwhelming desire for society; that is, for social life not of any and every sort, but peaceful, and organized according to the measure of intelligence.[12] They neither were nor are, by nature, wild unsociable beings. On the contrary, it is the corruption of their nature which makes them so.[13] Further, if humans are naturally social, their natural sociability should be protected against acts which destroy peace in society, such as the violation of others' property. Laws established to provide an order in society are thus not merely conventional, but have their basis in human sociability. The law of nature, as it appears from the *Prolegomena*, is the law which conforms with the social nature of humans and the preservation of social order; the law which applies to all humans. To its sphere belong such rules as not taking that which belongs to another, the restoration of damage, the obligation to fulfill promises, the reparation of injury, and the right to inflict penalties.[14] It exists independently of any will and cannot be changed by any authority whatsoever, whether divine or human.

Human natural inclination to one another, sociability or fellowship – in short, human social nature and not mere expediency – is the foundation of natural law: "a dictate of right reason which points out that an act, according to whether it is or is not in conformity with rational nature, has in it a quality of moral baseness or moral necessity."[15] Nevertheless, insofar as we have all been created weak, and lack many things needed to live properly, laws which have their ultimate source in human sociability are reinforced by expediency.[16] Grotius divides law into natural law and volitional law. Positive volitional laws, which emanate from the power of the state but have their ultimate point of reference in natural law, have always some advantage in view. Insofar as they are based on citizens' choice and consent, the laws of each state have in view the benefit of the whole society. For this reason, he argues, it is wrong to ridicule justice as folly. A citizen who obeys the law is not foolish, "even though, out of regard for that law, he may be obliged to forgo certain things advantageous for himself."[17] By violating a law of his country in order to maximize utility and obtain immediate advantage, the individual destroys the common welfare, by which the advantages of himself and his posterity are secured. The same applies to international law that has in view "the advantage, not of particular states, but of the great society of states."[18]

Grotius replaces the double standard of conduct for states in their internal affairs and in their foreign affairs, characteristic of politics of *raison d'état*, with a clear-cut parallelism. The conduct of nations is compared to the conduct of individuals. The "nation is not foolish which does not press its own advantage to the point of disregarding the laws common to all countries."[19] Although law is not founded upon expediency alone, no state can disregard potential benefits of international cooperation. He stresses mutual interdependence of states. In a mutually interdependent world, there is no state so powerful that it may not some time need the help of others outside itself, either for purposes of trade, or even to ward off the forces of many foreign nations united against it.[20] No state is free to act unlawfully. In disobeying the law of nations because of temporary profit to itself, the state separates itself from international society and hence undermines the foundation of its own security.

Grotius challenges the view that laws are merely conventional and justice is a matter of mere expediency. He asserts the essential identity of legal and moral rules governing the conduct of states and individuals, and traces the source of these rules to the law of nature. He does not identify international law with natural law, since the latter represents a body of moral rules known to all civilized human beings, while the former is a body of rules that have been accepted as obligatory by the consent of all or many states. However, the law of nature is for him the ever-present source for supplementing the voluntary law of nations, and for judging its adequacy in the light of ethics and reason.[21] It provides criteria against which the mere will and practice of states can be measured. At the same time, he draws our attention to the utility of international law. While the proponents of the doctrine of *raison d'état* argue that state interests override customary moral rules and international norms, Grotius attempts to show that this way of looking at national interest is the equivalent of looking into the wrong end of a telescope. It establishes a false dichotomy between the interests of particular states and the interests of the whole international community. It fails to appreciate how important international norms are when it comes to the constitution of state interests. Even if no immediate advantage were to be derived from the keeping of the law, Grotius says, it would be a mark of wisdom, not of folly, to allow ourselves to be drawn towards that to which we feel our nature leads.[22] Respecting international law and promoting international order can bring long-term benefits to all nations.

Jus ad Bellum and Jus in Bello. For adherents of the doctrine of *raison d'état*, ethical and legal norms are suspended by the necessities (such as the necessity to survive or secure power) which states confront in international relations. The stern necessities of the state justify doing evil. In the affirmation of "reason of state," the claim to an unrestricted right to war is thus the most important. War becomes the right of sovereign states and the very symbol of their sovereignty. Moreover, since war is always an instrument of state policy, as Carl von Clausewitz pointed out, it is limited insofar as policy was limited; however, once a state decided to pursue a policy of conquest and was no longer prepared to be bound by any established norms, it would fight a total and unconstrained war.[23] Grotius disputes these views. For him, states are composed of individual human beings[24] – a basic reason why their behavior is not subject to impersonal forces of necessity but ultimately always depends upon human decisions. States are not disorderly crowds but associations. As such, they are, as a rule, governed by individuals who reach decisions after deliberations and are capable of forming judgments on ethical and legal issues confronting them. Moreover, since states are collections of persons, they are subordinated to natural law arising from the nature of man as a rational and as a social being.[25] Hence, their behavior is subject to limitations. To control and limit war is thus not inherently impossible. Grotius attempts to limit and restrain war in two ways: firstly, by his just war doctrine which puts severe limitations on the reasons for which war may be fought; secondly, by putting legal restraints on its conduct.[26] The two phrases: *jus ad bellum* (justice of war) and *jus in bello* (justice in war) refer respectively to these two cases.

There are three views concerning the legitimacy of war. Firstly, there is the pacifist view that no act of war is legitimate. Secondly, there is the militaristic or Machiavellian view that any war that benefits the state is legitimate. Thirdly, there is the legalistic or Grotian view that there is a distinction between just and unjust causes of war, and that some wars are therefore legitimate and others are not. The pacifist and militarist views are both inimical to international order. The former rejects the violence that is necessary to uphold international order against attempts to subvert it; the latter admits violence of a sort that destroys international order.[27] For Grotius, the use of force is in no way discordant with social human nature. "The right reason and the nature of society prohibit not all force," he says, "but only that which is repugnant to society, by depriving another of his right."[28] Convinced that there is a common law among nations, which is valid alike for war and in war, he attempts to provide an alternative against both extremes, pacifism and militarism, so that humankind may not believe either that nothing or anything is allowable.[29] He denies the state the right to resort to war except in pursuance of a just cause: "No other just cause for undertaking war can there be excepting injury received".[30] He limits the justifiable causes of war to defense, recovery of property, and inflicting of punishment. In addition, he devotes an entire chapter of the *De Jure Belli ac Pacis* to an enumeration of various causes of unjust war.[31] He accepts as a just cause of war neither the desire for richer lands nor the desire to rule others against their own will on the pretext that it is for their good. Wars can be justly waged neither against those who refuse to accept our ideology or religion nor err in its interpretation. Furthermore, in elaborating the right of self-defense, Grotius rejects the claims of the war of prevention. He claims that the notion that "the mere possibility of being attacked confers the right to attack is abhorrent to every principle of equity. Human life exists in such conditions that complete security is never guaranteed to us."[32] In another part of the book, he says plainly that to "authorize hostilities as a defensive measure, they must arise from the necessity which right apprehensions create: there must be a clear evidence not only of the power, but also of the intentions of the formidable state."[33]

In Book III of *De Jure Belli ac Pacis* Grotius discusses what was considered to be just in war under the law of nations of his day: killing and wounding enemies, devastating, acquiring captured goods, enslaving prisoners of war, and obtaining supreme governing power. However, he does not approve of these practices. In chapters 11-16, which include chapters on admonition of *temperamenta belli* (restraints on war), he aims at providing rules for minimizing bloodshed. First, he seeks to restrain the right to kill. He states that no one may be killed intentionally except as a just punishment or by necessity, when there is no other way to protect life or property. Next, he specifies the categories of people who may not be killed. These include such non-combatants as children, women (unless they are fighting in place of men), old men, members of the clergy, men of letters, farmers, merchants, and artisans. He also argues that the lives of those combatants who surrender unconditionally or beg for mercy, and thus no longer pose a threat, should be spared. Grotius's argument in respect of devastating and pillaging is similar. Devastation can be undertaken to reduce the strength of the enemy. But devastation for devastation's sake is absurd and should be avoided. It is not allowed if, as a result of occupation, the land and its produce are effectively withheld from the enemy. Grotius also insists that the powers involved in conflict should refrain from destroying works of art, especially those devoted to sacred purposes. He believes that reverence for things sacred requires that sacred buildings and their furnishing be preserved. 1To evaluate the value of *temperamenta* he does not only refer to the law of nature. He also supports his emphasis on moderation in war by a prudential argument.[34] To refrain from indiscriminate killing, and from destroying and pillaging property, he argues, increases the likeness of one's own victory by depriving the enemy of the great weapon of despair.

De Jure Belli ac Pacis was read widely in the European intellectual circles of the seventeenth and the eighteenth centuries, and must have then exerted some influence on the process by which the severity of war in Europe was mitigated. Many rules and basic ideas of the law of war established in the late ninetieth and early twentieth centuries, especially by the Hague and Geneva conventions, follow Grotius's restraints on the conduct of war. Nevertheless, his just war doctrine was not accepted in his day and for three centuries thereafter. Prior to the changes introduced to international law in the aftermath of the First World War, states had the right to resort to war not only to defend their legal rights, but also in order to destroy rights of other states. This idea of the unqualified prerogative of states to resort to war as an instrument of national policy was opposed by the just war tradition that denied the absolute right to war and differentiated between wars which, in law, were just and those which were not. Grotius made a significant contribution to this tradition.[35] In the Covenant of the League of Nations, established in 1919 by the Treaty of Versailles and dissolved in 1946, lawful resort to war was diminished for the League's member states. International law on the right to resort to war was further developed by the Kellogg-Briand Pact of 1928, outlawing war as an instrument of national policy, and the UN Chapter of 1945. The provisions of the UN Chapter, aiming at providing a system of collective security, extend beyond Grotius' position. However, they preserve his basic idea that states may use unilateral force only for the purpose of self-defense, and not for the pursuit of their foreign-policy objectives.

Human Rights and Intervention. Against advocates of the doctrine of *raison d'état* Grotius argues that "there is a common law among nations, valid for war and in war."[36] His contribution to international relations theory is the idea that the binding force of law can be preserved in an anarchic international environment. Thus, he lays foundations for a universal international order dedicated to peaceful cooperation between equal and mutually independent sovereign states. Nevertheless, in addition to promoting the rule of law in inter-state relations, Grotius sets before the international community another goal of protecting people from harm and of promoting the protection of basic human rights. In the chapter "On Punishments," he says:

> The fact must also be recognized that kings, and those who possess rights equal to kings, have the right of demanding punishments not only on account of injuries committed, against themselves or their subjects, but also on account of injuries which do not directly affect them but excessively violate the law of nature or of nations in regard to any persons whatsoever.[37]

Central to Grotius's thought about war is the insistence that private war, violence between families, groups or cities, is forbidden. "No war can be made but by the authority of the sovereign in each state."[38] Grotius is thus against non-state violence, and has been criticized because of his disapproval of the right of resistance to oppression. He asserts that a rebellion in the form of a war of liberation is not permitted under natural law. To recognize a right of resistance for him is contrary to the purpose for which the state is formed, that is, the maintenance of public peace (*De Jure* I, ch. 4, ii-v). Nevertheless, he adds to his position a few important qualifications. Right of popular resistance exists when rulers openly demonstrate themselves enemies of the whole people or attempt to usurp parts of sovereign power not belonging to them. Further, he permits non-violent struggle and defends such individual rights as the right to defend one's persons and property, the right to refuse to carry arms in an unjust or even morally doubtful war, and the right to purchase necessities of life, such as food, clothing or medicine, at a reasonable price (*De Jure* II, ch. 2, xix). He is also clearly ahead of his time when he discusses humanitarian intervention. Notwithstanding his reluctance to sanction wars of national liberation, he considers the prevention of the maltreatment by a state of its subjects a just reason for war.

Based on the notion of state sovereignty over its own territory, international law has traditionally opposed not only unilateral intervention in the domestic affairs of one country by another, but also collective action. The only exceptions are grave threats to the peace and security of other states and of egregious and potentially genocidal violations of human rights. While addressing the dilemma of whether the sovereignty of a state should be respected or the rights of the individuals within the state protected, Grotius offers a basic principle by which humanitarian intervention can be justified. He acknowledges the established rule that "every sovereign is supreme judge in his own kingdom and over his own subjects, in whose disputes no foreign power can justly interfere."[39] However, he argues that the state that is oppressive and egregiously violates basic human rights forfeits its moral claim to full sovereignty. When the rulers provoke their people to despair and resistance by unheard-of cruelties, having themselves abandoned all laws of nature, they lose the rights of independent sovereigns and can no longer claim the privilege of the law of nations. Humanitarian intervention is therefore for Grotius a kind of international equivalent of domestic law enforcement. Governments that engage in acts that allow other states to intervene in their domestic affairs for humanitarian purposes are considered by him to be criminal governments. While Grotius generally denies the oppressed the right of resistance, he permits a foreign state to intervene, through war, on their behalf. "Admitting that it would be fraught with the greatest dangers if the subjects were allowed to redress grievances by force of arms, it does not necessarily follow that other powers are prohibited from giving them assistance when laboring under grievous oppression."[40]

Grotius argument for intervention is based on the assumption of one common nature which humans have and which alone is sufficient to oblige people to assist each other. Human social and rational nature is the source of natural law, and a foundation of human rights. In the sense that pertains to an individual human being, "right (*ius*) is a moral quality, annexed to the person, justly entitling him to possess some particular privilege, or to perform particular acts."[41] Although Grotius's list of human rights violations and barbaric acts may be different from today's, he asserts as a mater of principle that members of the international community are not obliged to respect the sovereignty of a state which engages in acts of cruelty and violates human rights. Whoever commits a crime, whether a criminal individual or a criminal nation, by the very act can be considered to fall into the level of brutes and can be regarded as inferior to anyone else.[42] Those human beings that break basic rules of humanity and renounce natural law are wild beasts rather than humans, and against them a just war can be fought. "The most savage war is against savage beasts, the next against men who are like beasts."[43] However, Grotius does not license intervention everywhere to everyone, and qualifies his argument with prudential considerations. Since a state's own existence and preservation is the object of greater value and prior consideration than the welfare and security of other states, "no one is bound to give assistance or protection when it will be attended with evident danger."[44] In his view, national responsibility, the obligation of the government to its own citizens, is regarded as most important, and it takes precedence before cosmopolitan responsibility for all humans. Our common nature, he suggests, tells us that if possible something should be done to stop human suffering on a mass scale wherever it occurs. But governments should always protect their own people first and avoid taking unnecessary risks with their welfare; only then can they try to help whomever else they can. "No ally is bound to assist in the prosecution of schemes which afford no possible prospect of a happy termination."[45] Intervention is justified only if the military risk is not high and there is a reasonable chance of success.

Political realists are critical of intervention, arguing that states act only when it is in their interest to do so. They argue that disregarding the rights of sovereignty of other states to promote human rights may lead to an undermining of peace and order. Grotius does not deny self-interest in international politics. However, he believes that states can identify their interests not only with narrow national goals but also with a greater task of the preservation of international order.[46] In such case, cosmopolitan responsibility for other humans and the rogue states punishment (especially in situations where human rights violations result in grave threats to peace for neighboring states) is not contrary to national interest. Nevertheless, as a word of warning, Grotius says that "wars which are undertaken to inflict punishment are under suspicion of being unjust, unless crimes are very atrocious and evident."[47] The danger that a humanitarian intervention can be used as the cover of ambitious designs, "by which no faults of kings but their power and authority will be assailed," cannot be completely removed. "But right does not lose its nature from being in the hands of wicked men."[48] Grotius anticipates the idea, which underlies the system of collective security of the United Nations, that to avoid the situation that under a pretended humanitarian intervention there will be an interest of a single state to undertake a military action against another, the process of judgment whether or not to undertake such action must be multinational.[49] Collectively approved action can correct for self-interested interventions covered by a thin cloak of humanitarianism.

Old and New Challenges to the Grotian Order. Under Grotius's influence, international law changed its old meaning of a set of customs which were discovered to be common to the juridical practice of many different peoples, to a body of rules regulating the relations between sovereign states. He posited the idea of the international rule of law, even in warfare, and thus provided the foundation for a universal legal order applicable to all nations, an order whose purpose is to encourage cooperation between states and reduce the risk of a conflict arising among them. Yet, just as his ideas were frequently discussed, quoted, and admired, they were also fiercely attacked and described as utopian or unrealistic. Not only his idea of international legal order but also his concept of fixed moral standards derived from natural law, by which policies and political actions could be judged, have been challenged.

The initial challenge came from Hobbes, Grotius's younger contemporary. Although he does not mention Grotius by name, in his *Leviathan*, first published in 1651, Hobbes makes a formidable attack on the views underlying Grotius lifework. He argues that there is no society between states because there is no common power, authority, and law; that states have an absolute and unlimited sovereign power and, as a matter of sovereign prerogative, are entitled to wage war; that their mutual relations appear to be those of perpetual conflict; that going to war is simply striving to enforce our will as a people on another people; that peace is only a breathing time; that ethical norms do not hold at war and consequently crimes during war do not exist. Hobbes joins the camp to those who dismiss the idea of international norms founded on natural law. In different ways, Machiavellians, Hobbesians, Hegelians, and Marxists all agree.

By subjecting Grotius's ideas to criticism, Hobbes voiced the prevailing international practice of governments of his day. In many cases these ideas were read in a way that were contrary to Grotius's own intentions. Grotius was praised equally by hawks and doves.

His ideas could gratify the high-minded because they sounded lofty and pointed out a way which could reasonably lead to a more peaceful world, while in practice, they could not restrict the struggle for power between European states and their endeavor to subject non-European people to their authority.[50] Grotius's just war doctrine was all too often used instrumentally by hard-liners and militarists to justify the right to start war. His right to intervention provided too readily a pretext for brigands of all kinds to subjugate foreign peoples.

The age of Grotius was the time of national arms build-up, not arms restriction. The era of colonial conquests by European nations had just begun. But the problem remains. At its core lie important questions. Under what conditions can states punish another state or undertake a humanitarian intervention? Can rules and norms of international society provide restraint against the potential egoism of states? Do they contribute to greater cooperation and peace among states? Are rules and norms merely an expression of a particular interpretation of national or class interests at a particular time?

The value of Grotius's work is not that it provides answers to all these questions. He is, however, an important voice in the debate about the character of international politics. He wrestled with problems which continue to concern us. It is his conviction that people do not conduct their foreign policies independently of their cultural values. The international legal order which he envisions is not compatible with societies in which the individual human being is not recognized as the primary principle, but is reduced to a member of a tribe, a nation, or a class; in which the essential elements that constitute human nature, human rationality and sociability, are not recognized; and in which natural law is either not acknowledged or not understood as a moral law. Those core values and norms of Western civilization have been under a constant threat of militaristic ideologies. Upon their sustenance, the future of the present Grotian global order, based on rule of law in international relations, ultimately depends.[51]

NOTES

1. Quentin Skinner, *The Foundations of Modern Political Thought*, Vol. 1 (Cambridge: Cambridge University Press, 1978), 248.
2. On the influence of Machiavelli's thought on Frederick the Great and other statesmen, and on the development of the doctrine *raison d'état* by philosophers Fichte and Hegel, and German historians such as Leopold von Ranke and Heinrich von Treitschke, see: Friedrich Meinecke, *Machiavellism: The Doctrine of Raison d'État in Modern History*, Trans. Douglas Scott (New Brunswick, N.J.: Transaction Publishers, 1998).
3. Greg Russell, *Hans J. Morgenthau and the Ethics of American Statecraft* (Baton Rouge: Luisiana State UP, 1990), 9.
4. *Prol.* § 22. My citations from *De Jure Belli ac Pacis* are taken from the English translation by Francis W. Kelsey of the Latin edition of 1646. This translation forms part of the series "The Classics of International Law," published by the Carnegie Endowment for International Peace. Kelsey' translation was published in 1925.
5. *Prol.* § 3.
6. *Prol.* § 5.
7. *Prol.* § 22.
8. *Prol.* § 5.
9. Reinhold Niebuhr, *The Children of Light and the Children of Darkness: A Vindication of Democracy and a Critique of Its Traditional Defense* (New York: Charles Scriber's Sons, 1960), 8.
10. *Prol.* § 7.
11. *De Jure* 1,1,11. I follow a standard form of reference (book, chapter, section).
12. *Prol.* § 6.

13. *De Jure* 1, 1, 12.
14. *Prol.* § 6.
15. *De Jure* 3, 11, 16.
16. *Prol.* § 16.
17. *Prol.* § 18.
18. *Prol.* § 17.
19. *Prol.* § 18.
20. *Prol.* § 22.
21. H. Lauterpacht, "The Grotian Tradition in International Law," *British Yearbook for International Law*, 23 (1946): 1-53. Rpt. in *Grotius*, Vol. 1, Ed. John Dunn and Ian Harris, *Great Political Thinkers*, Vol. 7 (Cheltenham: Edward Edgar, 1997), 396-448.
22. *Prol.* § 18.
23. Michael Howard, ed. *Restraints on War: Studies in the Limitation of Armed Conflict* (Oxford: Oxford University Press, 1995), 6.
24. *De Jure* Book 2, 1, 17.
25. *Prol.* § 26.
26. *Prol.* § 25.
27. Hedley Bull, "The Grotian Conception of International Society," *Diplomatic Investigations: Essays in the Theory of International Politics*, Ed. Herbert Butterfield and Martin Wight (London: Allen and Uwin, 1966), 54.
28. *De Jure* 1, 2, 1.
29. *Prol.* § 29.
30. *De Jure* 2, 1, 1.
31. *De Jure* 2, 12.
32. *De Jure* 2, 1, 17.
33. *De Jure* 2, 22, 5.
34. *De Jure* 3, 12, 8.

35. See G. I. A. D. Draper, "Grotius' Place in the Development of Legal Ideas about War," *Hugo Grotius and International Relations*, Ed. Hedley Bull, Benedict Kingsbury, and Adam Roberts (Oxford: Clarendon, 1990), 202.
36. *Prol.* § 24.
37. *De Jure* 2, 20, 40.
38. *De Jure* 1, 3, 5.
39. *De Jure* 2, 25, 8.
40. *De Jure* 2, 25, 6.
41. *De Jure* 1, 1, 4.
42. *De Jure* 2, 20, 3.
43. *De Jure* 2, 20, 40.
44. *De Jure* 2, 25, 7.
45. *De Jure* 2, 25, 4.
46. *Prol.* § 17.
47. *De Jure* 2, 20, 43.
48. *De Jure* 2, 25, 8.
49. Micheal J. Smith, "Humanitarian Intervention: An Overview of the Ethical Issues," *Ethics and International Affairs: A Reader*, 2nd ed. (Washington, D.C.: Georgetown University Press, 1999), 291.
50. B. V. A. Röling, "Are Grotius' Ideas Obsolete in an Expanded World?," *Hugo Grotius and International Relations*, Ed. Hedley Bull, Benedict Kingsbury, and Adam Roberts (Oxford: Clarendon, 1990), 297.
51. This text was originally published under the title "In Defense of International Order: Grotius' Critique of Machiavellism," *The Review of Metaphysics* 60 (September 2006), pp. 55-70.

8. On Freedom from Hate

> Nonviolence is not a mere philosophical principle. It is the rule and breath of my life. It is a matter not of the intellect but of the heart. — *Mahatma Gandhi*

August 31st marks the anniversary of the end of prolonged strikes in the Gdansk Shipyard which resulted in the forming of the Independent Self-Governing Trade Union "Solidarity" in Poland. The peaceful resistance and ethics of Solidarity still remain a powerful lesson in political non-violence. It was the persistent, non-violent political struggle of Solidarity in the 1980s that consequently led to the downfall of communism in Central and Eastern Europe in 1989 and to dramatic changes that followed all over the world.

Solidarity (in Polish "Solidarnosc"), a trade union and an independent social movement, was born in August 1980 after mass strikes which swept all over Poland. However, in spite of the wide support it enjoyed in Polish society, it was outlawed in December 1981 and its leaders were imprisoned. If one is suppressed by force, one can answer with force. One has a right to defend oneself.

The right to self-preservation has been recognized as a fundamental right of an individual, but also of society. Why did Solidarity not answer force with force? Was that an ethical standpoint that Solidarity used peaceful means only in its defense or a utilitarian or pragmatic strategy? Before I answer these questions, I shall first make some remarks about the nature of the communist political system which existed in Poland after the World War II. Thus, I wish to point out the sources of injustice that existed in that country. As a response to this injustice, Solidarity arose.

Social Conflict in Classless Society. An underlying feature of the political system that existed in the People's Republic of Poland from 1945 to 1989 was the presence of communist ideology. In light of this ideology private ownership of the means of production was abolished. Polish society was declared to be a classless society in which there was no place for social conflict.[1] It was believed that conflicts and contradictions between social classes, such as between the owners and the employees, would arise from the fact that the former desired more profit and robbed the latter of the full fruit of their labor. Such conflicts would no longer hold in a classless society, in which there was public ownership of the means of production, and everyone who worked was supposed to be an employee and an owner at the same time.

The results of social conflicts are strikes and demonstrations. There were several cases of strikes and demonstrations in the People's Republic of Poland. They seemed to contradict the ideological theory. This is why in Poland, in a supposedly classless society, the word "strike" was forbidden. If there was a strike in a factory or an institution, it was called a "work-interruption" by state-controlled mass media. Likewise, any protest march or demonstration was called a "disturbance." Thus, the presence of the theoretical concepts of Marxist-Leninist philosophy, namely, communist ideology, in light of which there should be no conflicts in a classless society, distorted the facts. It made facts nonexistent.

Perhaps the greatest thing that the ideology concealed was the fact that Polish society of the 1950's-1980's, a society of so called "real socialism," was a society with real and inherent social contradictions. The supposedly class society was in truth torn apart by conflicts of interests, not of those who were owners and those who were employees, but of those who held power and those who were controlled. The one-party system and the lack of separation of power, which were characteristic not only of Poland, but of all communist-ruled countries, led to an enormous concentration of power in a few hands. A classless society was thus in fact not classless at all, but characterized by at least two classes, namely, the *apparatchiks* who held power, and those who were controlled. The popular participation in power, like the elections, were only an illusion. The governments of East European countries which hold power against the will of the majority of their citizens were ironically called "People's Republics" or "People's Democracies". A hierarchical class society built along the rigid lines of the economic, social, and political inequalities between those who control and those who were controlled, was called "classless society."

Because of the enormous concentration of power, on the one hand, and its absence on the other, the communist-ruled countries were endangered by a condition of internal conflict to a degree higher than any of the Western democracies in which there is a separation and checking of power. This explains why the communists developed a vast apparatus of repression, ready to silence any voice that might attempt to challenge their power. Yet, every act of repression was also a step that led the oppressed people to realize that that lived in an oppressive kind of regime. Every act of repression aiming at the preservation of an oppressive regime was also, paradoxically, a step leading to its downfall.

Concentration and centralization of power, bureaucratization of its execution, and the manipulation of public opinion, so as to distort the facts, were characteristic of the regime of the People's

Republic of Poland. It was also characterized by the oppressive means employed for the sake of its preservation.

The Burden of Freedom. It may be astonishing for someone to hear that people do not always desire freedom. They often exchange freedom for security, satisfaction of material goals, or a quiet life. They may thus very well accept regimes that take away from them the responsibility or burden of freedom. In other words, they may let others guide their own lives, and lose almost all powers to participate actively in the decision-making process. In such instances, the best that may be said is that they are governed with consent, but the means of bringing about this consent are often those of suggestion and manipulation. Yet, if there are such people, there are also others, "freedom seekers," those who, in contrast to the former, not only ask whether their life is a good one, but also challenge the life prescribed to them by their administrators. Such people actually take the burden of freedom upon their shoulders. Further, if there is an ideology that assumes that the life which it prescribes is the best one, then a conflict must inevitably follow between the "freedom seekers" and the authority. In the face of oppression, the former may withdraw from taking responsibility for their lives, submit to the force of authority and live under suppression. Still, this will not discourage some others, who will persist in their questioning.

In Poland under the communist regime there was a long list of questions which Polish citizens wanted to ask, but in general were afraid to do so. Some of these questions concerned the criminal way in which the communists seized the political power in Poland.[2] There were questions about Katyn Forest,[3] Yalta, and the Home Army, the most powerful Polish underground military organization fighting against the Nazi German occupation, whose members were systematically persecuted and often killed by the communists after the II World War. However, there were also pressing questions concerning basic economic needs. All workers' protests in Poland would always begin with simple economic questions and then they would eventually inspire questions concerning social and political issues, proceeding beyond the mere economic.[4] Hence, in postwar Poland, the majority of society, even if they wanted to, could not exchange freedom for security or material satisfaction because there was none. With the exception of some periods of greater stabilization, the economic questions have always been acute and the government incapable of solving them, so there was great dissatisfaction with the regime among a large part of society.

Injustice can be defined as undeserved suffering. People who work hard for small salaries, whose views and questions are silenced, and who if protest, are persecuted, are subjected to injustice. They do not associate their vision of a good life with the life they are actually living. Upon realizing that he is being subjected to injustice, an oppressed person will try to eliminate it. This is how social change may occur. Yet, he must know the sources of injustice. He must understand why is he oppressed and who the oppressor is. This is where the function of political opposition comes about. It is political opposition that prepares the ground for a mass political struggle.

Before 1976, groups of intellectuals had occasionally protested state policies in Poland, but there was no organized opposition movement.[5] Shocked by the brutal repression of workers' protests against price hikes in June 1976, a small group of intellectuals organized the "Committee for the Defense of the Workers" (Polish acronym KOR).[6] This first dissident organization was soon joined by others: "The Movement for the Defense of the Rights of Man and Citizen" (ROPCIO), "The Movement of Young Poland" (RMP), and "Confederation of Independent Poland" (KPN). In addition, a large underground press and the "Association for Scholarly Courses" (TKN), an underground educational organization.

The Church supported dissident activities.[7] It was a very joyful day for many people in Poland when on 16 October 1978, Cardinal

Karol Wojtyla, the former Archbishop of Krakow, was elected Pope and took the name of John Paul II. His election strengthened not only the position of the Church in Poland, but also the dissidents. The Pope's first visit to Poland in June 1979 had a tremendous impact on the country. Thousands gathered to attend his open air mass in Warsaw; about one million came to hear him at the Polish national shrine in Jasna Gora; and about two millions heard him in the open fields outside Krakow. John Paul II spoke openly about the right to freedom. Years of communism seemed to vanish overnight as people gathered in millions to listen to and to cheer their Pope. The barrier of fear was broken.

The mass demonstration of Polish Catholicism in June 1979, was a prelude to the birth of Solidarity in August 1980. Four years after the emergence of an organized opposition in Poland and one year after Pope John Paul II's first visit to his home, Polish society was ready to renounce its obedience to the communist regime.[8] Polish citizens would in the 1970's taste a little bit of freedom and as a consequence their desire for freedom became even more strong. The Independent Self-Governing Trade Union "Solidarity" sprang up when people in Poland gained desire for freedom on such a wide scale that in a few weeks in the summer of 1980, within the country of thirty-five million citizens, an independent union of ten million working people was born. First, the workers' protests of 1956, then the student demonstrations of 1968, then the ruthlessly suppressed workers' protests of 1970 and 1976 – all these events were the precursors of the famous strikes of 1980, when for the first time in the history of Communism, the most revolutionary class according to Marx, namely, the workers, decided to end the very political system that was inspired by his philosophy.[9] Never before Solidarity were the inherent contradictions of a communist-ruled country seen so clearly.

The Glorious Birth. For several days in the summer o 1980 the eyes of the entire world were focused on the Gdansk Shipyard, on the masses of people and their cry for freedom. Foreign observers were shocked by the peaceful nature of the strike.[10] On August 31, 1980 the government signed an agreement with the worker's representatives (the Strike Committee). The Gdansk agreement known as "21 Points" marked the birth of Solidarity, a free trade union and an independent social movement.[11] There were at least four distinct phenomena connected with the birth of Solidarity.

First, there was the transformation of the goals of the worker's struggle. The mere economic demands transformed into social and political issues. The striking workers demanded not only better salaries, but also freedom for political opposition and respect for human rights. While most of the 21 points of the Gdansk agreement dealt with such social and economic matters such as wages, working conditions, or health insurance, its core was political. It contained provisions for the workers' right to form free trade unions and the right to strike; and it dealt with such issues as freeing political prisoners, the legal definition of censorship (i.e., the passing of a law to this effect), and trade unions' access to the mass media.

Second, there was institutionalization of the struggle. The worker's protests of 1956 and 1970, although they led to some political changes in Poland, including changes of government, could not have a long-term influence on political life because there was no organization or institution which would defend the conquests won during the struggle. It was finally in August 1980 that there arose a popular recognition that to defend the gains of the protests, an institution was needed, namely, the Independent Self-Governing Trade Union "Solidarity."

Third, in August 1980, Polish society was for the first time truly united. Solidarity, the outcome of the August strikes, was an institution whose members were simple workmen, as well as university professors and members of the Academy of Sciences; activists of political opposition, as well as popular actresses and actors. The majority of Polish society became united by the program of economic, social, and political reforms of Solidarity.

Finally, there was a lack of ideology. Solidarity had not been an outcome of any particular social theory or philosophy. The intellectual disputes about it began after it was born. Solidarity arose rather as a result of popular recognition of certain basic human needs, such as food, as well as truth and justice, a recognition that grew in Poland through the years following World War II.[12] It should be stressed that the lack of ideology, which would precede the birth of Solidarity, was the result of the complete bankruptcy of communist ideology in the eyes of the prevalent part of Polish society. With an ideology, there is always a dogma connected. People in Poland had a first hand experience of the harmful consequences of the dogmas of Marxism-Leninism.

Why did the government give in and sign the 21 points? It was afraid of a massive uprising all over Poland, so it wanted to gain time. But from the moment Solidarity was born, the Polish party leaders began to draw up plans to crush it.[13] Their monopoly threatened, the communist authorities were unable to come to terms with the independent trade union. Initially, Solidarity wanted to act within the limits of normal trade union activities. However, the external conditions imposed on it by the totalitarian system, in which there was no competing political parties, forced the union to exceed these limits by proposing to the government several reforms in education, law and economy, as well by supporting the independent organizations and institutions which, born along with Solidarity, were unable to defend themselves against party-state oppression.

The Imposition of Violence. On 13 December 1981, the state attacked the society. Several thousand Solidarity activists were imprisoned, censorship of correspondence was implemented, and travel around the country limited. The imposition of martial law in Poland is still surrounded by a controversy.[14] Was it to save the country from a direct military intervention of the USSR? But was there a real danger of such intervention?[15] In any case, imposed efficiently by Polish hands, martial law provided the best solution for the Soviets, considering the risk and possible harmful political consequences of a direct intervention. Its imposition was thus in the Soviet interest.

With the approval of Moscow, by imposing martial law, the party-state apparatus decided on the tactic of terror because it represented an insignificant part of Polish society and was unable to otherwise impose its will on the majority. The ten million Solidarity members, along with members of Rural Solidarity and other independent organizations, such as the Independent Association of Students, together with their families, constituted the vast majority of the population of Poland. Less than one hundred thousand specially selected police and military forces were able to terrorize the movement of millions of unarmed, peaceful people. The question now to be raised is: Why did Solidarity not respond with violence against violence directed towards it?

The most obvious answer is that Solidarity was never, nor attempted to be, a military organization. Furthermore, in spite of all confrontation with the authorities during 1980-1981, there was always hope on the part of the majority of Solidarity's leaders that a dialogue with authorities, finding of a common ground and a common body of interests, was possible. In spite of all the economic, social and political demands which it made, Solidarity of 1980-1981 did not want to take over the power of the state, but rather to be a check on this power, so as to prevent it from being misused.

The belief in the possibility of dialogue with authorities made Solidarity completely unprepared to defend itself in case of a violent confrontation. The only form of defense was a total strike. And indeed, thousands of enterprises went on strike in order to protest the imposition of martial law. All these strikes were broken by force. The iron gates of Gdansk Shipyard were torn apart by tanks and workers returned to work. The only place where the workers defended themselves by force were two Silesian mines, "Wujek" and "Jastrzebie." At the coal mine "Wujek" the workers used fire extinguishers and metal tools against the police armed with weapons. Seven of them were tragically killed and the strike was broken.

The answer that Solidarity was not prepared for a violent resistance would, however, be all too simple. The popular image of Solidarity was at the time so high that of three million party members, at least one third joined Solidarity. These were mostly ordinary working people. Further, this high image went beyond the working people, reaching as far as the military and police forces. In 1981, a Solidarity cell was formed within the police. However, it was not officially recognized by the authorities. Consequently, one can suppose that if on the part of Solidarity leaders there was a call to defend oneself by force, there would be mass resistance, and at least some military and police forces would be prepared to support the position of Solidarity. Yet there was no such call. The striking workers were asked not to resist and to surrender to force.

Principle and Pragmatism. The forming of Solidarity in August 1980 was a spontaneous act on the part of the people who, in common, had learned from the mistakes of the past crises in Poland, of 1956, 1968, 1970 and 1976. However, by December 1981 Solidarity had became a well organized institution guided by a large body of its leaders and advisers, as well as a coordinated social movement. The peaceful response to violence was then a conscious act of Solidarity's leaders. Was this an ethical decision or a pragmatic choice?

In order to answer this question we need, for a moment, to look at Polish history. The last two centuries were for Poland indeed full of suffering. By the end of the eighteenth century the country was divided between three powers of Russia, Prussia and Austria. The history of Poland in the nineteenth century is marked by desperate attempts to regain national independence, and particularly by the November 1830 and January 1863 insurrections against Russia, both ruthlessly suppressed. It was only because Polish refugees of the nineteenth century found suitable conditions outside Poland, especially in France, that Polish national consciousness and culture were cultivated independently, outside the annexing countries. In the twentieth century World War II had completely changed the picture of Poland, which, for the twenty-year period between the First and Second World Wars enjoyed again full independence and very prosperous development. Six million Polish citizens were killed during the war, including three million ethnic Poles. [16] Cities, villages, and the country's infrastructure were to a large degree destroyed. Again, during World War II there were desperate attempts to liberate the country. Poland had an extensive and well organized underground.[17] The Polish Army operating on both Western and Eastern fronts was fourth in terms of strength and number in the anti-German coalition. The courage and dedication of Polish people had contributed to the victory of the Allied Forces over Nazi Germany, but the pact signed in February 1945 in Yalta sealed the country' fate.[18] Poland had fallen into the sway of communism. Consequently, the war was a painful lesson, especially the Warsaw uprising of 1944, after which the city was raised to the ground and thousands of innocent civilians killed. This is the price of violent resistance. The greatest tragedy is evident when, in spite of all dedication, suffering and blood, the political goals are not achieved. Then such a resistance remains an example of patriotism and heroism, but also a painful lesson for future generations.

Indubitably the painful lesson of Polish history teaches that one always should calculate whether or not violent military resistance can be successful. Such resistance is always connected with the possibility that it could be bloodily suppressed, and thus bring more harm than good. The consideration of Solidarity leaders that violent resistance to martial law, instead of improving the situation in Poland, might lead only to the death of the most dedicated and patriotic people was certainly sufficient for making the decision not to resist force and to surrender. By not resisting the force against which one cannot defend oneself, one hopes to preserve one's life. Thus, he/she makes a pragmatic or tactical move. One does not renounce his/her ideas, but only suspends their practical implementation for a period of time.

However, the nonviolent political struggle of Solidarity was not only guided by pragmatic considerations of how to achieve the goals more effectively, but also by ethical principles. Solidarity of the 1980s was a mass movement based in a society in which traditional Christian values were still very much alive – even among those people who did not regularly go to church.[19] The transformation of the goals of the worker's struggle which occurred during the August strikes, from economic demands to social and political issues, had gone even further and can be rendered as a desire to replace lies with truth and to free oneself from hate. Therefore, there is a grave moral content that can be assigned to Solidarity on an equal basis with the economic, social and political reforms. Solidarity can rightly be called a movement of renewed morality because such traditional notions as truth, justice and freedom, ridiculed once in the *Communist Manifesto* and distorted in the practice of communism, have because of it found again their original meanings.

Freedom from Hate. In the *Informational Bulletin "Solidarnosc,"*[20] published in Gdansk on 19 January 1981, there was an article by Mariusz Wilk entitled "Wolnosc od nienawisci" (Freedom from Hate). In this article, he wrote:

There is a peculiar change, a phenomenon that has occurred simultaneously with the economic, social, political and cultural changes initiated in recent months by Solidarity. I shall call this change a movement towards freedom. By freedom, I hereby understand an act of releasing oneself from hate. This is for me the greatest conquest of August 1981.

And he writes further:

> Totalitarianism poisons with hate both those who are its followers and those who resist it. One can neither conquer nor resist totalitarianism, one can only overcome it. Liberation from hate is also a liberation from passivity to solidarity. This is again the greatest achievement of Polish society since World War II.

On 24 April 1986, Mariusz Wilk, then thirty-three years old, former editor of the *Informational Bulletin* of Solidarity, the co-author of the underground best-seller entitled *Konspira*,[21] was arrested and charged with violating Act 132, that is, cooperation with a foreign organization whose activities are harmful to the state. Evidence for this charge was a copy of a contract with an Italian publisher for publication of *Konspira*, found during a police search at his home. He was kept in a cell without much light, apparently to harm his sight. He was released during the September 1986 amnesty.

If one uses force against another, the latter has a right to defend himself. Yet, he may stand beyond the level of hate and retaliation. Thus, he consciously accepts the principles that have been handed down by the Christian ethical tradition. These principles are still very much alive in Poland and this is a second answer as to why Solidarity was not a violent movement.

Conclusion: A Turning Point in our History. Looking from today's perspective, the tactics and ethics of Solidarity, employed for the sake of political struggle in the 1980s, have proved to be the right ones. After new waves of strikes in 1988, the newly appointed government, taking advantage of the reformist trends introduced in the USSR by Mikhail Gorbachev, took steps to liberalize the economy and opened dialogue with the political opposition.[22] The so-called Round Table Talks, on the conditions of a peaceful reform of the political system, started in February 1989, lasted for two months and resulted in a constitutionally defined agreement to move toward democracy. Solidarity was restored as a legal organization. In June 1989 the first partially free elections were held. Solidarity's Citizens Committees gained 35 percent of the First Chamber seats (the other 65 percent was reserved for the communists (PZPR) and their coalition partners). Even so, the communists failed to produce the majority because their partners, the puppet peasant and democratic parties, switched sides and lined up with Solidarity. In the Senate, 99 out of 100 seats went to Solidarity. In September 1989 the first non-communist government in a former Soviet satellite state was formed.

The sudden and unexpected collapse of Communism in 1989 in Poland and in other countries of Central and Eastern Europe, often symbolized by the fall of the Berlin Wall, took even close observers of the region by complete surprise. The breakthrough made by Solidarity paved the way for some of the most significant events in the recent world history. It has led to the institution of democracy in several countries, the dissolution of the Soviet Union and the birth of new states, the reunification of Germany, the enlargement of NATO and the expansion of the EU. It has resulted in dramatic political, economic, and cultural changes that followed all over the world. In the aftermath, different interpretations of what happened were made, the most common being that communism could not compete economically with democracy, and as a result between 1989 and 1991 most of the former communist countries abandoned that system.[23] But, as today's examples of North Korea, China, Cuba, and other countries can show, economics by itself could not crush such a powerful ideology as communism, which has a high degree of persistence and can adapt itself to the changing international environment. The turning point of history was the series of events that took place nine years earlier, in August

1980, when Solidarity was born at the Gdansk Shipyard. Without the birth of Solidarity, there would have been no fall of the Berlin Wall. The Gdansk Shipyard, in which massive strikes and other forms of peaceful resistance were initiated, became the place that inspired the rest of Poland with freedom, and Poland soon began to have a similar effect on other countries of Central and Eastern Europe. The birth of Solidarity was the crack in the structure of the Soviet Block that began the end of the totalitarian system.[24]

NOTES

1. See Stanislaw Starski, *Class Struggle in Classless Poland* (Boston: South End Press, 1982).
2. See Krystyna Kersten, *The Establishment of Communist Rule in Poland, 1943-1948*, trans. by John Micgiel and Michael H. Bernhard (Berkeley, California: University of California Press, 1991); Stefan Korbonski, *Warsaw in Chains* (New York: Macmillan Co., 1959), Stanislaw Mikolajczyk, *The Rape of Poland: The Pattern of Soviet Aggression* (Westport, Conn.: Greenwood Press, 1972).
3. The name Katyn stands for the best known of the three places of the execution by the NKVD, in spring 1940, of 14552 Polish officers, prisoners of war. They were murdered at Katyn, Kalinin/Tver and Kharkov. See Allen Paul, *Katyn: The Untold Story of Stalin's Polish massacre* (New York, N.Y.: Maxwell Macmillan, 1991); Solomon W. Slowes, *The Road to Katyn: A Soldier's Story* (Oxford: Blackwell, 1992); Robert Szymczak, "A Matter of Honor: Polonia and the Congressional Investigation of the Katyn Forest Massacre," *Polish American Studies*, 41 (1) Spring 1984, pp. 25-65; J. K. Zawodny, *Death in the Forest: The Story of the Katyn Forest Massacre* (Notre Dame, IN: University of Notre Dame Press, 1962); *Katyn. Documents of Genocide: Documents and Materials from the*

Soviet Archives turned over to Poland on October 14, 1992, trans. and ed. Wojciech Materski, Foreword by J. K. Zawodny (Warsaw: Institute of Political Sciences, 1993).

4. See Jane Leftwitch Curry and Luba Fajfer, *Poland's Permanent Revolutions: Peoples vs. Elites, 1956 to the Present* (Washington, D.C.: American University Press, 1996).
5. On the background to August 1980, see Michael H. Bernhard, *The Origins of Democratiziation in Poland.: Workers, Intellectuals and Oppositional Politics, 1976-1980,* (New York, N.Y.: Columbia University Press, 1993); Keith John Lepak, *Prelude to Solidarity: Poland and the Politics of the Gierek Regime* (New York, N.Y.: Columbia University Press, 1988).
6. Jan Jozef Lipski, *KOR : a History of the Workers' Defense Committee in Poland, 1976-1981*, translated by Olga Amsterdamska and Gene M. Moore (Berkeley, California: University of California Press, 1985).
7. See Bogdan Szajkowski, *Next to God -Poland: Politics and Religion in Contemporary Poland* (London : F. Pinter, 1983).
8. There are several reasons why Solidarity was born. One of them was certainly the strength of the Catholic Church in Poland and the election of Cardinal Wojtyla to the Holy See. In spite of many attempts Communist were never able to suppress the Church and to impose a complete ideological domination over Polish society. Christian values would provide an intellectual defense against values of historical materialism. Another important reason was a relative liberalization in Poland in the 1970's. Edward Gierek, who became the Party leader after in December 1970 workers' protests in Gdansk and Gdynia were brutally suppressed by force, promised that violence would not be used against workers again. During the 1970's Poland became a relatively open and prosperous

country. Gierek tried to obtain Western loans and to improve Polish economy. Polish citizens, especially university students, would begin to travel freely to the West. Although it was subjected to some repression, there was a powerful underground press. In 1975 Poland signed the Helsinki Agreement, on the basis of which it was obliged to respect human rights and fundamental freedoms, including the freedom of thought, conscience, religion or belief, and this fact would give additional protection and moral strength to the political opposition. Last but not least, one of the key reasons was Poland's history and her ancient republican traditions, deeply rooted in the Polish soul.

9. On political developments in Poland, see Curry and Fajfer, *Poland's Permanent Revolutions*; Jakub Karpinski, *Countdown: the Polish Upheavals of 1956, 1968, 1970, 1976, 1980*, translated by Olga Amsterdamska and Gene M. Moore (New York: Karz-Cohl, 1982); Gale Stokes, ed., *From Stalinism to Pluralism: A Documentary History of Eastern Europe since 1945* (New York: Oxford University Press, 1991).

10. For the best eyewitness account of a foreign journalist, see Timothy Garton Ash, *The Polish Revolution: Solidarity* (New York: Viking Penguin, 1991).

11. On the August strikes and negotiations in the Gdansk Shipyard, see Neal Ascherson, *The Polish August: The Self-Limiting Revolution* (New York: Viking Press, 1981); A. Kemp-Welch, *The Birth of Solidarity. The Gdansk Negotiations, 1980* (New York: St. Martins Press, 1983).

12. On the rise of Solidarity, see Lawrence Goodwyn, *Breaking the Barrier: The Rise of Solidarity in Poland* (New York: Oxford University Press, 1991); Jan Kubik, *The Power of Symbols against the Symbols of Power: The Rise of Solidarity and the*

Fall of State Socialism in Poland (University Park, Pa: Pennsylvania State University Press, 1994); Roman Laba, *The Roots of Solidarity: A Political Sociology of Poland's Working-Class Democratization* (Princeton, N.J.: Princeton University Press, 1991).

13. On Solidarity's Challenge in 1980-1981, see Nicholas G. Andrews, *Poland 1980-81: Solidarity versus the Party* (Washington, D.C.: National Defense University Press, 1985); Peter Raina, *Poland 1981. Towards Social Renewal*, (Boston: G. Allen & Unwin, 1985); Kevin Ruane, *The Polish Challenge* (London: BBC, 1982); Jadwiga Staniszkis, *Poland's Self-Limiting Revolution* (Princeton, N.J.: Princeton University Press, 1984); Alain Touraine, *Solidarity: The Analysis of a Social Movement. Poland 1980-81,* trans. by David Denby (Cambridge: Cambridge University Press, 1983).

14. On martial law in Poland, see chs. 5-7 in Werner G. Hahn, *Democracy in a Communist Party: Poland's Experience since 1980* (New York, Columbia University Press, 1987); Jan Mur, *A Prisoner of Martial Law: Poland, 1981-1982*, trans. by Lillian Vallee (San Diego : Harcourt Brace Jovanovich, 1984); Leopold Labedz, ed., *Poland Under Jaruzelski*, (New York: Scribner, 1984).

15. Tatiana Zonova, whose paper was presented at the conference on "Dissent and Opposition in Poland," organized by Centro Studi sulla Storia dell\'Europa Orientale (CSSEO), Trento, Italy, December 2005, made an archive research on the meetings of the *Politbiuro* of the Communist Party of the USSR from years 1980-1981. The conclusion of her research presented at the conference was that the Soviet Communist Party leaders would stress absolute impossibility of Soviet direct intervention in Poland. At the same time, they would discuss ways how to scare the Polish public opinion by organizing Soviet military manouvers next to the Polish border

and would try to exert a pressure on General Jaruzelski, who was then the leader of the Polish Communist Party. They drafted a plan of the martial law to be implemented by Polish hands. This confirms an earlier research made by Rudolf Pistoja, former director of the Soviet archives. See a chapter on Solidarity from Rudolf Pichoja's book, *Sowietskij Sojuz - istorija w³asti. 1945-1991*, Moskwa 1998. This chapter was translated into Polish as "Dwie Solidarnoœci: socjalistyczna i polska" and published in *Zeszyty Historyczne*, vol. 132 (2000).

16. On crimes against Polish population, see Szymon Dater, *War Crimes in Poland's Genocide 1939-1945* (Poznan: Wydawnictwo Zachodnie, 1962); Richard C. Lucas, *The Forgotten Holocaust: The Poles under German Occupation, 1939-1944* (Lousville, K.Y., University Press of Kentucky, 1986).
17. See Stefan Korbonski, *The Polish Underground State: A Guide to the Underground 1939-1944*, trans. by Marta Erdman, (New York: Columbia University Press, 1978).
18. See John L. Harper, Andrew Parlin, *The Polish Question During World War II* (Washington, D.C.: Foreign Policy Institute, 1990); Jan Karski, *The Great Powers and Poland 1919-1945:* from Versailles to Yalta (Lanham, M.D.: University Press of America, 1985).
19. On Solidarity's peaceful resistance in 1982-1988, see Grzegorz Ekiert, *The State Against Society: Political Crises and Their Aftermath in East Central Europe,* (Princeton, N.J.: Princeton University Press, 1996); Michael T. Kaufman, *Mad Dreams, Saving Graces. Poland: A Nation in Conspiracy* (New York: Random House, 1989); John Rensenbrink, *Poland Challenges a Divided World*, (Baton Rouge, Louisiana State University Press, 1988).

20. In Polish *Biuletyn Informacyjny "Solidarnosc."* Translations of the quotations below are my own.
21. Maciej Lopinski, Marcin Moskit and Mariusz Wilk, *Konspira. Solidarity Underground*, trans. by Jane Cave, (Berkeley, California: University of California Press, 1990).
22. See Jadwiga Staniszkis, *The Dynamics of the Breakthrough in Eastern Europe. The Polish Experience,* trans. by Chester A. Kisiel (Berkeley, California: University of California Press, 1991).
23. Tom Lansford, *Communism* (New York, NY: Marshall Cavendish Benchmark, 2008), p.83.
24. An earlier version of this paper was published in *Journal of Human Values*, vol. 8.1 (2002), pp. 57-66.

9. Righteousness of Life

> If you are not being educated to life, then education has no meaning. — *J. Krishnamurti*

In the grim picture of politics in the twentieth century there are not many moments of light. Solidarity is one of them, not only because it stood for such fundamental human values as freedom and justice, and was victorious, but also because it earned its victory in a non-violent way. It initiated a profound world transformation. Today we live in a world that is fundamentally different from that before 1989. We are no longer divided by a global ideological struggle between communism and liberal democracy. The key issue today is not a bipolar division, but globalization. The collapse of communism has made the world almost into one single market. In addition, an expanding global system of communication, especially the Internet, has helped to establish a single global society. At the same time, the world today is affected by serious problems. There are tensions and violent conflicts in many parts of the world, and we are haunted by the danger of terrorism and war. There is a grave poverty problem all around the globe. There is massive cross-border crime. Finally, there are environmental challenges, such as pollution and shortage of water and global warming.

Globalization, poverty, crime, terrorism, scarcity of resources, environmental pollution, global warming: these are the issues that in one way or another affect human beings today. They influence human life in a powerful, often destructive way. They necessitate a new positive world transformation and a new solidarity that can undertake it. Is such a transformation possible? What can the new Global Solidarity learn from Poland's Solidarity?

From Poland's to Global Solidarity. There were four factors connected with the birth of Solidarity.[1] First, economic demands were transformed into social and political issues. Second, there was institutionalization of the struggle. Third, in August 1980, Polish society was for the first time truly united. Fourth, there was the lack of ideology. If we could then apply these factors to today's Global Solidarity, it would have to be a global civic movement, based not on any ideology, but rather on the recognition of some fundamental human needs, having the ability to unite around its program a large portion of global society, and capable of becoming an efficient institution. Like Poland's Solidarity movement it would uphold the needs of all, notwithstanding human differences. Moreover, it would be guided by the idea of non-violence in obtaining social and political goals. It would exert pressure on governments to implement reforms that would facilitate a world transformation. Whether Global Solidarity will be established on the basis of some existing NGOs that share a similar program and can become something like an umbrella organization for them, or will be a new establishment, is a technical question that is not going to be discussed here. The World Civil Forum, which took place in Seoul in May 2009, and brought representatives of many civic organizations from all over the world, could, in fact, be the first step in establishing Global

Solidarity and promoting a world transformation.[2] Again, is such a transformation possible?

Inclusive Values and the Righteousness of Life. The world has escaped a global confrontation between communism and liberal democracy, and possible nuclear annihilation, but it continues to be divided—not only by economic and political differences, but also by differences in religion and culture. Conflict is a part of the reality of life, but it is not its essence as political realists claim. If life was only conflict, then nothing would ever grow. Growth, and not conflict, is the essence of life. Ideologies of all sorts try to hamper the process of growth and arrest time, by claiming that they represent the end of history, but time will always free itself and life will finally prevail. Positive world transformation is about minimizing conflict and averting the danger of war, protecting life, and allowing life to flourish.

Global Solidarity presupposes human fellowship, a unity that comes out of diversity, and, like Poland's Solidarity after 1989, is destroyed by discord. In the world of so many conflicting ideas and interests can such a fellowship be ever achieved and maintained?

In spite of all their differences, human beings are able to recognize their basic needs. Food, shelter, family, and safety are needs whose recognition comes from life itself. They constitute inclusive values—values that unite and do not divide, and that people coming from different cultures can acknowledge as their own. It is true that some people may forsake family and safety, and embrace solitude, adventure, and risk to obtain some goals. Solitude, adventure, and risk can indeed be a way of life, but on them life cannot be build. The same applies to conflict and war. They can be a way of life, or a part of life, and yet we cannot construct life on them. The normal process of growth requires peace. Furthermore, the development of individuals does not only necessitate the basic human needs, such as food, shelter, family, and security, but also liberty and respect. Freedom has a great value if it enhances life, but it loses its value if it turns against life. Individuals cannot develop intellectually without freedom. They also cannot be fully satisfied in life without recognition from others and without friendship. Life is not merely about physiological processes. Human life includes full psychological development, and this can be achieved only in certain conditions. Poverty, malnutrition, enmity, disrespect, injustice, violence, as well as ideas that are destructive to life, reduce our chances of becoming well-developed individuals.

Cultures, religions, ideologies, nationalities, particular interests: they all divide us. Let us find a common ground. This is life itself. The institution of Global Solidarity depends on the recognition of some fundamental human needs that are indispensable, not only for life but also for fulfilled life. Many of these needs have been described as internationally recognized human rights. The *Universal Declaration of Human Rights* lists such rights as "freedom from hunger," "adequate standard of living," and "liberty and security of person." However, whereas rights are entitlements and imply that a claim can be made against some party, needs of life or inclusive values derived from them do not have such a legal connotation. They imply knowledge of the essence of human life. Global Solidarity is not based on legal claims but on the growing common understanding of what is right for life. It is based on the righteousness of life.

The Common Interest in What is Right for Life. Politics is a part of life. It involves interests and power, but politics cannot be reduced to a mere power game. It is a mixture of ideas and forces. Poland's Solidarity defined itself against the Soviet totalitarian system. It was finally achieved when people, freeing themselves from propaganda, got the idea of what was right for their lives, and when they became interested and determined enough to put this idea into practice. But when communism collapsed, the commonality of their interest was quickly replaced by the particularity of group and individual interests, and Solidarity disintegrated. Life in Poland, and elsewhere, went forward, but only half way. Similarly, the understanding of what is right for life is essential but not enough for building a Global Solidarity movement. In addition to the knowledge of the righteousness of life there must also be a common interest in bringing what is right into practice by a large portion of global society.

Life is the central concept around which humanity can unite. Global Solidarity defines itself against those theories and practices of today that are destructive of life, especially against, ideological materialism, political totalitarianism, religious fundamentalism on the one hand, and crime, terrorism and militarism, on the other.

Ideological materialism is destructive to life because of its simplified picture of life that is reduced to its mere physiological, mechanistic or violent aspect. For the materialists life is merely a pursuit of pleasures and material goals, and its mechanics can be reduced to the conflict of interests. This deviated picture of life dominates a substantial part of the tradition of political realism, into which students of politics and its practitioners are socialized, and is recaptured in thousands of today's books and movies, whose chief subject is violence. It is also present in the positivist social sciences and critical social theories. Such a picture of life does not allow for any true human solidarity.

Political totalitarianism and religious fundamentalism are destructive to life because they deny human beings the freedom of questioning and unlimited inquiry, and impose on human lives their dogmatic interpretations.

Crime is destructive to life for it directly brings harm to its victims and degrades human beings. Sex trafficking and trafficking in human organs are the darkest sides of globalization.

Terrorism and militarism are directly destructive to life because they imply no respect for life whatsoever. Those who are engaged in these practices are the most removed from the idea of human fellowship. Wars may be fought in the defense of life, but never against life.

Solidarity, Community and Global Governance. Global Solidarity can be achieved if there is a growing recognition of what is right for life and a growing interest in protecting and enhancing life. Its foundation is provided by global society, whose members are all the human inhabitants of earth, but its institution does not endanger the existence of communities at the national and local levels. Not only are those communities important for life for they provide their members with opportunities to express life in different forms, but also they are important instruments of security. The decline of bonds that unite people at a national level and the erosion of states' sovereignty which are the results of globalization cause an increase in crime. Failed and internally weak states become havens for criminals and terrorists. Therefore, it is a mistake to think that states are no longer relevant in today's global environment, and that they should be removed and replaced by a centralized world government. There is no guarantee whatsoever that such a system of government would perform its function any better than the present state system, when it is inspired by the ideas of cooperation, multilateralism, and the rule of law, promoted by the United Nations.[3] It will certainly not eradicate the problem of human conflict and violence. Like Poland's Solidarity movement which has never aspired to become a government, Global Solidarity does not necessitate a new global authority. That has, in a limited form, already been provided by the UN.

The actual picture of the world is too complex to be reduced to simple ideological dichotomies of the oppressors and the oppressed, of the rich and the poor, or of those who are satisfied with their power and those who are not. It includes both old and new threats such as poverty, crime, religious and ethnic conflict, terrorism, global warming, energy scarcity, and so on. These threats are magnified by the widening spread and quickening pace of globalization. To deal effectively with them, one has to work on many levels of governance. Instead of weakening or denying the state, we should make it stronger internally, but at the same time more responsible to other states and more interdependent. This can be achieved by building of international society based on the UN and other international organizations. States that are linked to others by international institutional and economic ties are important focal points of security and community.

The weakness of international organizations in the past was that the national governments, especially of great powers, would not support them. As a result many resolutions and initiatives that could potentially benefit humankind could not be put in practice. For example, the American withdrawal from the Kyoto Protocol in March 2001, during the George W. Bush administration, did incalculable damage to the efforts of the international community to construct a unified response to the global warming threat—the damage that will hopefully be repaired by Barack Obama. In order to minimize such unilateral and potentially damaging responses to world problems by individual state actors moved by their national self-interests, Global Solidarity would exert pressure on governments, so that they support international organizations and implement reforms that would facilitate a positive world transformation. At the same time it would also make initiatives of its own and propose them to international organizations. While wielding power that at present none of the NGOs represent, it would be a life promoting and enhancing instrument of global society through which a more humane world could be achieved.

× × ×

There are different communities and social levels at which individuals can relate to each other: family, local community, nation, and global society. These communities serve various functions in human life and; therefore, they all have their validity. Global society can replace neither family nor nation, but it adds a new element to them, namely humanitarian responsibility. It postulates that, in addition to being a responsible family member and citizen, one should also feel responsible for what happens to any other human being who lives on earth; that one should neither do harm to others nor be indifferent to other peoples' suffering. Global Solidarity requires more. It obliges us to defend and enhance life against those forces that are destructive of life, and to exert pressure on governments, so that they support international organizations and consider the welfare of all humanity. Global Solidarity calls us to be guided by the righteousness of life.

NOTES

1. See the previous chapter: "Freedom from Hate."
2. This chapter is a revised version of the paper that was presented at a World Civic Forum session devoted to "Global Peace and Global Governance."
3. Kofi Annan, "Five Lessons I Learned as UN Secretary-General," *New World*, Jan-March 2007, pp. 18-21.

10. All is One

> If you wish to make good efforts then change your thoughts. Create very quiet and silent thoughts. You can make the quality of your thoughts very good; very pure.
>
> —*Dadi Janki*

The saying of Heraclius, "Listening not to me but to the Logos, it is wise to agree that All things are One" (Fragment 50), can be understood at least in two senses. First, the saying provides us with an exposition of the meaning of the Logos. Second, through it we receive advice from Heraclitus on how we can better understand our-own-being-in-the-world.

In order to grasp properly the meaning of the Logos, we must realize that the ancient Greek word is derived from the root *legein* (gather, collect). There is also another meaning of *legein*, namely, talking or saying. However, in fragment 50, Heraclitus asks us not to listen to him, to his talking but to the Logos. "All things are one," or rather, "All is One" is that with which one who listens to the Logos agrees. By truly listening to the Logos, we can experience a unity of All in One. The Logos is thus explained as the One throughout which the All is being brought together.

"All is One" (*hen panta einai*) can also be translated as "One is All." On the one hand, everything is revealed in the One (All is One): the universe discloses itself in one who is attuned to the Logos. On the other hand, the One is revealed in everything (One is All): not only is the world is revealed in one, but one also reveals himself in the universe and thus finds his own place in this world.

You could not in your going find the ends of the soul, through you traveled the whole way—so deep is its Logos (Fragment 45).

The simple saying: "All is One; One is All" itself attunes and engages us with the Logos. In the Logos, Heraclitus has expressed the unceasing human search for oneself, for the meaning of the human-being-in-this-world that can be regarded as the ever elusive knowledge of the whole.[1]

NOTES

1. Fragments of an unpublished manuscript entitled "Logos and Wonder."